Notting Hill Ponces

Tommy Kennedy IV

NEW HAVEN PUBLISHING LTD

Published 2020
NEW HAVEN PUBLISHING LTD
www.newhavenpublishingltd.com
newhavenpublishing@gmail.com

Front cover design © Alan Blizzard
Back cover design @Pete Cunliffe

Acknowledgements

Firstly, I would like to thank all the readers who bought my last book, *Nightmare in Jamaica*, and thank the new readers. Without you giving me the encouragement to carry on writing I would never have finished both books.

Anna Carrington, for her vision for this book, and Jay Hirano, for the inspiration he gave me to write anything at all. I am also grateful to Janice Stretton for encouragement and guidance. My childhood friends Robert Albert Taylor, AKA the Rat, Malcolm Lawless, AKA Tank, and Kenny Fearon are all now deceased: 'See you on the other side muckers.'

All my Japanese friends: Mona, Haruki, Mai who taught me true manners. I hope to get to Japan one day for sure. Alan Clayton from the Dirty Strangers, Brummie Mick for all the great laughs and escapades over the years. Frank and the gang, Allison, Sandra, Sarah, Del, Maz, Steve, Lucinda.

I'd like to thank all the staff at the Mau Mau Bar. My daughter Sophie and her three beautiful children, Barclay, Theodore, and Penelope, and my 12-year-old son Tommy Junior V.

I would like to give a shout out to all the bands I have been involved with over the years, especially around the Notting Hill area, some I managed, some I promoted. All of them taught me something, in one way or the other. Over a twenty year period here are just a few - there were way too many to mention them all - NRG-FLY, Steve Dior Band, Pink Cigar, The Electrics, Kult 45s, Dirty Strangers, Stolen Colours, Carnival of Souls, Angie Brown, Killing Joe Band, Freak Elite, Smiley and the Underclass, Slydigs Warrington, Mentona K, from Liberia, Rotten Hill Gang, Whalls, Etchoo Band, Serratone Warrington, Taurus Trakker, London Ghost, Alabama3, Alan Wass R.I.P, Ted Key and the Kingstons, Black Swan Event, Midnight Poem, Healthy Junkies, The SD5, Brady Bunch, Garage Flowers, Santa Semeli and the

Monks, Guinea Pigs of 37 Meta Data, Stanlees, The Stage Invaders, My Drug Hell, Anarchist 38 Wood, Slow Faction, Relaxin Doves, The Loves, David Sinclair Four, Prisoners of Mother England, Albie Deluca, Sugar Lady from Holland, Big Mackoofy, Anna Pigalle and Nick Farr, Aunty Puss, Raindogs, Paper Rock, Ray Hanson, The Vulz, Dave Renegade, Pistol Head, Bexatron, Chubby Letouche and his Band of Whores, Natural Mystery Museum, Jem and Helenna, Dave and Paolo, Key Mcloud, DJs, Alex Pink, Dr Philgood and Naughty Di, Steve Holloway, Rude Boy Ray Gange.

'Rock 'n' Roll saves lives'

It was the sudden realisation that my luck could run out at any time that made me pen my life story; it was a fire at my flat in London that almost claimed my life and gave me pause for thought.

I just thought: 'If I don't write it now, I'm never going to write it.' So I just got stuck into it.

Introduction

Welcome readers! We meet again.

In our last meeting you will recall that I had endured a harrowing 3-year prison sentence in the General Penitentiary of Jamaica. To those of you whom I am meeting for the first time I would advise you to buy the first bloody book!

To recap: I had survived a series of painful life changing events which caused a great deal of introspection and consternation, all of which I shared with you. We parted company in 2003 when I flew back to the UK.

Here, I am introducing you to my second and final volume of autobiography where I relate my experiences in London's Notting Hill. You will explore the creative community where I have lived for many years. You will meet a rich variety of people who have had to work extremely hard to survive; some are famous people, but most are not, but they all live in their individual creative bubbles. In fact, many continue to live their lives in a way reminiscent of the traditional starving artists, transported to the 21st century.

The title of the book, *Notting Hill Ponces*, in a lighthearted way requires explanation for the more uninitiated amongst you. The definition of 'ponce' is, 'To behave in a posh or effeminate manner, to borrow (something) from somebody without returning it.' It was back then a joke between musicians who were constantly blagging and 'poncing' off each other in the form of free drinks or free clothes; in short, getting things for nothing! We were all guilty of it, unless you were rich that is. It is, I realise now, part of the rich tapestry of the life I led back then.

Finally, the community spirit and camaraderie in this book has supported me through many of my most difficult experiences. This work serves as a personal tribute to those memories, and the people who I was privileged to meet in that crazy but special time in my life.

'Desiderata - Words for Life'

'Go placidly amid the noise and haste and remember what peace there may be in silence. As far as possible without surrender be on good terms with all persons. Speak your truth quietly and clearly; and listen to others, even the dull and the ignorant; they too have their story. Avoid loud and aggressive persons, they are vexations to the spirit. If you compare yourself with others, you may become vain and bitter; for always there will be greater and lesser persons than yourself. Enjoy your achievements as well as your plans. Keep interested in your own career, however humble; it is a real possession in the changing fortunes of time. Exercise caution in your business affairs, for the world is full of trickery. But let this not blind you to what virtue there is; many persons strive for high ideals; and everywhere life is full of heroism. Be yourself. Especially, do not feign affection. Neither be cynical about love; for in the face of all aridity and disenchantment, it is as perennial as the grass. Take kindly the counsel of the years, gracefully surrendering the things of youth. Nurture strength of spirit to shield you in sudden misfortune. But do not distress yourself with dark imaginings. Many fears are born of fatigue and loneliness. Beyond a wholesome discipline, be gentle with yourself. You are a child of the universe, no less than the trees and the stars; you have a right to be here. And whether it is clear to you, no doubt the universe is unfolding as it should. Therefore, be at peace with God, whatever you conceive Him to be, and whatever your labors and aspirations, in the noisy confusion of life, keep peace with your soul. With all its sham, drudgery, and broken dreams, it is still a beautiful world. Be cheerful. Strive to be happy.'
                                                    - Max Ehrmann

This is a true story of real sex, real rock 'n' roll, and real people.
                        Portobello Road, Notting Hill.

Chapter One

'All the world's a stage, and all the men and women merely players. They have their exits and their entrances, and one man in his time plays many parts.'

- William Shakespeare

Summer Of 2003 - Once Upon A Line

I was made up to be leaving Brixton and getting a roof over my head in Notting Hill. I liked Brixton but I knew a lot more people in West London. Since leaving the Penitentiary in Jamaica I was genuinely enjoying my freedom, and everything felt slightly surreal; getting used to the sights and sounds of freedom took some adjusting to, but I lapped it up with relish. I was now 43 years old and felt my life was ready to have fun.

Brixton is a district of South London, England, within the London Borough of Lambeth. It is mainly residential with a prominent street market and substantial retail sector. It is a multiethnic community, with a large percentage of its population of Afro-Caribbean descent. It lies within Inner South London and is bordered by Stockwell, Clapham, Streatham, Camberwell, Tulse Hill, Balham, and Herne Hill. The district houses the main offices of the London Borough of Lambeth.

I threw what clothes I had into a bin bag, headed down the stairs of Carrot's flat and made my way to the tube station in Brixton, passing the crack heads who were out in force this morning. I was glad to know I had somewhere to go. 'On with the next adventure,' I thought. I caught the Victoria Line to Oxford Circus and changed there for the Central Line to Notting Hill. I was squeezed in tight with the morning rush hour crowd and was glad when I got off at Notting Hill tube station and wandered down

Portobello Road to find my new lodgings on Westbourne Park Road.

It was starting to rain so I quickened my pace, passing the tourists going about their shopping looking for a bargain, just killing time before they flew home. I heard a lot of Italian accents; they seemed to flock over here in the summer months. It took me about 20 minutes to reach Westbourne Park Road and find my new lodgings. I walked up the steps and looked to see which bell to press. I rang the bell.

My new landlord Tony buzzed me up. I went up a couple of flights of stairs and he called from a room, 'I'm in here.' I entered his room; it was full of antiques and he had a rocking horse stood in the corner. The room was large and spacious and had a homely feel about it; I could tell he liked the finer things of life. Tony asked if I wanted a coffee, and I said, 'Yes, one sugar please.' We sat around chatting, drinking the coffee, and he explained it was £50 a week, and he would collect the rent each Friday night. Ok, this was a great deal and I was incredibly happy to be here. After we finished chatting, he took me up to the top floor of the house and showed me my room, gave me the keys, and left me to it.

Moving into Tony's was a blessing. After being kicked out of the gaff in Brixton I could have been on the street. I made the room comfortable, set my books up on a table in the corner, and made up the bed.

I had never met Tony before. He was around 5ft 10, mixed race, and had a scar on his right cheek. He was friendly; he was good friends with my friend Rob, so we got off on a good footing, luckily for me: there is nothing worse than moving in with someone who is moody as fuck. He knew everybody and most people knew him, so I had landed on my feet really. Tony was a man after my own heart, intelligent, a heart of gold, born and bred around the Grove, and better still, the local drug dealer. Fuck, we hit it off from the moment we met!

The Royal Borough of Kensington and Chelsea is an Inner London borough with royal status. It is the smallest borough in London and the second smallest district in England; it is one of the most densely populated administrative regions in the United

Kingdom. It includes affluent areas such as Notting Hill, Kensington, South Kensington, Chelsea, and Knightsbridge.

God it was so good to be home and free, and back in Notting Hill. The Queen's English was spoken in the Royal Borough of Kensington and Chelsea, along with hundreds of other languages, of course; all kinds of people had made their way to the global capital, which had been built and plundered by the East India Company, who over the centuries had brought vast amounts of money back to the heart of the Great British Empire, and built one of the most exclusive boroughs in the whole of London, and indeed the world.

The slave trade between Britain, Africa, and the Americas transformed the economy of Britain as an industry, and commerce flourished on the back of its success. The processing and distribution of products such as tobacco, sugar, and cotton produced on plantations resulted in massive investment in British quaysides, warehouses, factories, trading houses, and banks. The profits built fashionable townhouses and rural stately homes for the masters of the trade in London, which grew as the slave colonies became more important.

A few days later I made my way along to the Post Office to deliver my letters and parcel.

When I was walking around the streets when they first released me from the Penitentiary in Jamaica, I would have to pinch myself that I was here, and not in some dream I was having. It had affected me so much; I was so glad to be back and far away from that house of horrors where I nearly lost my life and sanity.

Beneath the glitz and the glamour, Notting Hill was a place which Irish navvies and immigrants from around the Empire had helped to build with their toil, blood, and sweat; and they in time made Notting Hill their home, and ended up living in the hovels around North Kensington.

I felt at home and deeply appreciated my freedom on these walks of discovery, catching up with what I had missed over the years.

They had been hard men from a bygone era, who usually had large families themselves, and were often involved in murders and drugs, stretching back over a hundred years, long before the film *Notting Hill* brought in the oligarchs and bankers from places like the US, Russia, China and all the super-rich from every country you could think of. You can see how wealthy parts of the Borough are, just by looking at the buildings. I was soaking up the atmosphere and felt like I had won the lottery, strolling around bumping into people I knew. I heard a familiar voice. 'Hello Tommy, good to see you back,' said Geordie Jimmy from across the road. 'Nice one Jimmy, great to be back.' I carried on walking, all the time feeling like a free man, and thinking about the white middle classes who proclaimed they were from 'Notting Hill, darling,' situated close by to Heathrow Airport. The drugs that came in by their tons were often plentiful and distributed around the rest of the country; the original County Lines. The wealthy population went about their businesses blissfully unaware of what was going on around them, unless of course they fancied a line of the heavenly white powder that fed their egos, and made them fuck like animals; then they would be supplied by one of the local gangs who worked on their patch close by to their large houses; then the two worlds met.

Just before I went to jail in Jamaica, I noticed how much cocaine was being flooded onto the streets of London. By the year 2000, crack and cocaine use was increasing in the UK. It was being used as far south as Jersey and as far north as Aberdeen. It has spread to injecting users and is now also being distributed through heroin dealing networks. It is also gaining popularity within the dance drug culture/bars and clubs. Seventeen years after its introduction to the UK it is still marginalised as a drug with regards to treatment and national strategy.

By the time I got out in 2003, crack and cocaine use was now beginning to be taken seriously by various government departments such as the NTA, the Home Office, and the Cabinet Office. This is helping to ensure that the issue is discussed and thought about. However, the stereotypes and myths surrounding the use of this drug continue to interfere with the development of rational policies and practice.

I remembered all the deals that went on around these very salubrious streets, taking in everything and missing nothing on my stroll.

The real Notting Hill is a fascinating place to be, surrounded by council estates, populated by people who are as down to earth and sharp as razors, used to hustling and working and trading close by to the world-famous Portobello Road Market, or as the locals call it, the Bella. I sometimes felt like I was on a film set, which indeed it had been a few years before when the film *Notting Hill* had been made.

I knew a lot of people in the area, and a lot of people knew me through my musical endeavours, which I had put on over the years before I went to prison. The fake people will always eventually reveal themselves, as indeed do the genuine ones who could make me laugh and feel good and at ease in their company.

I had been surrounded by killers in Jamaica, and you quickly learn how to read people under those circumstances. It was so good to be back, at long last a free man. I had dreamt of these streets for so long: a place that welcomes people from all over the planet. I slotted back in no problem; it was as if I had never been gone. I carried on with my walk heading towards the Post Office to send my letters and the parcel to the Penitentiary in Jamaica.

When I had left the General Penitentiary I had promised Aljoe and Leppo I would write and send them some CDs. So I bought some from the record stalls on Portobello Road. Leppo loved reggae, and Aljoe the old delta blues. I had written each of them a letter a few days before, saying I was glad to be back in London, and for them to take care of themselves. I arrived at the Post Office and parcelled the CDs up, licked the stamps, and sealed the box. As a former prisoner you are not supposed to correspond with other prisoners. I hoped they would get them. I gave the parcel to the postmaster to be weighed, and paid for the delivery to Jamaica. I had already written my address on the back of the envelope.

Leaving the Post Office, I just hoped they would receive them back in Jamaica.

I often thought about them, but never really held out much hope that Aljoe would be released for the terrible murders he had committed when he had been a boy of 17. I knew Aljoe could barely read and write, even though he was a genius on guitar.

I had also written a letter to Dennis Lobban, AKA Leppo, who was serving life for the murder of reggae superstar Peter Tosh and his friends. He had always proclaimed his innocence, but who really knew what happened on that fateful night back on the 11th September 1987?

Peter M Tosh, OM (born Winston Hubert McIntosh; 19 October 1944 – 11 September 1987) was a Jamaican reggae musician. Along with Bob Marley and Bunny Wailer, he was one of the core members of the band the Wailers (1963–1976), after which he established himself as a successful solo artist and a promoter of Rastafari. He was murdered in 1987 during a home invasion.

I had investigated Leppo's case and saw that his fate had been well and truly sealed by reading the news reports of the day. When I left in 2003, he had been in prison for over 16 years. This was what he was saying in 2003 when I left. The popular theory was that Lobban killed Tosh because Tosh reneged on an agreement between them. While not wanting to go into too much in detail, he admits 'I took a rap for my bredren, protecting his career, and nothing has been done for me, and they say that I get corrupted and assassinate him because he never pays any attention to my kids and my family, and things like that.' However, he says that he cannot see why that would be used as a reason to convict him. 'If you are going to do something for a bredren to protect his career, why is it that when something like this happens now, they are going to use it?'

That stint Lobban refers to was his second time in prison. He had been there before as a 16-year-old student at Denham Town Secondary. He says he was wrongfully imprisoned, on a suspicion of larceny charge. Lobban says that these days he does not get many visitors, because the people who do come are his family, but they live abroad. His friends, he says, have admitted that they would come to visit him, but do not want people to know that they are his friends. He now spends his time writing and performing dub poetry, reading books, and listening to the news. 'I have nothing against the society because I was told to forgive, so I also forget everything,' he says. Naturally, he has hopes of leaving prison, but through the proper channels. 'I am not going to go jump no wall. I want to walk through the gate. I need to go and live some life now with my family.' *The Jamaican Star* 2003

As I write this now, Leppo, has been in the General Penitentiary 33 years with still no hope of being released soon.

'Out of adversity comes opportunity'
                                    - Benjamin Franklin

My mind was made up. I was a man on a mission, a musical mission. I was putting my life on hold, for better or worse I was going to give it my best shot or die trying. Mentona K from Liberia had disappeared; Rudi, the South African singer, had turned his back on me, disgusted that I had been arrested for drug smuggling. He had been based in Germany with my spiritual guru, Rike, but they split, and he went back to South Africa. Oh well, I would carry on and find new bands.

Arriving back at Tony's I went up to my room and started reading. My mind was wandering, and I put the book down and started plotting and planning my next move over the coming weeks and months that lay ahead.

I had met Billy Idle when he was working with Howard Marks. He lived over in Kensal Green. Billy was running the Bankers Draught pub in Kensal Rise when I first came back from Jamaica, so I thought I would go over and see about putting gigs on in his pub. He agreed and we worked out a deal. I got to know a lot of his friends from those days; Jay Kelly from Manchester, and Mick the Scouser. They were all up for a laugh.

Billy had been a doorman in the Hacienda back in the day. He was also a DJ and played all over. He worked a lot with the infamous Rotten Hill Gang. He had turned into a Buddhist after living in Thailand years before, giving up booze and becoming a vegan. Originally from Little Hulton in Salford, he had grown up with Shaun Ryder from the Happy Mondays and was well connected with the music fraternity in Manchester. I would see him a lot around London at gigs and we were good friends. He was just under six feet and had an enormous moustache with a beard, and dressed like he was from the 1930s. He had his own style and it suited him.

He was a good man to turn to for advice as well: he always seemed to have an angle on any problem you might have, and how to resolve it. I used to go and have a spliff with him now and then. There was a great community vibe around where he lived. The women loved Billy and he loved the women. It was always good to run into him.

I began to put on gigs anywhere and everywhere that had a stage, around West London and beyond. I was like a man possessed, running up and down Portobello Road dropping flyers and talking to people who had shops, asking if I could put posters in their windows. I was a one-man-band and there was nothing I didn't do or wasn't prepared to do, in promoting gigs.

I ran into a young band called Carnival of Souls, who I had met before my incarceration. I knew the singer Gronk, and the guitarist Gus. They had both been pupils at Eton. I had never met anybody who had been to such a school, but we hit it off. They were about eighteen and had been playing loads of gigs all over London; they had a large following of young people in the area, and they put on great shows with a good atmosphere. So we did a few shows together and I got to meet a lot more musicians. Gus was more the business type, and played lead guitar, and Gronk was the singer and played keyboards. Within a few months they moved out of the area though, over to East London into a warehouse, and I never saw that much of them after that, for a while.

When I was younger my grandmother used to tell me, 'When you get older, surround yourself with young people, they will keep you inspired and on your toes.' I never really planned for it, but it was unfurling that way. I didn't want to sit in pubs chatting shit and talking about yesteryear. I was winging my way through life and having fun; I was alive and free.

I was running into dealers around the pubs and clubs of London, supplying E and coke predominantly; it was the party drug of choice. Heroin was being done at home; the smackheads preferred that, gorging on the golden-brown, flaked out, talking of their big plans that never amounted to anything after they came down, and they would be out chasing the next score to numb the pain of withdrawals.

The Moroccans were dealing the finest hashes over the Golborne Road end of Portobello, and the Columbians were dealing the coke out of North Kensington. You would often see them gliding by in their black Mercedes with blacked-out windows; 'I've got a ticket to ride.'

The Spaniards were coming in their droves with suitcases stuffed with every conceivable hash you could think of, low key people trundling along with multiple kilos, moving and selling to the ever-growing population of the borough; you could buy anything. The streets were alive with punters ever willing to part with cash for the best products. Well, I thought, I am out of the game, I will look to make my money elsewhere.

Was I tempted? I was, but still I soldiered on with the music, and I met everybody who was passing through, Scousers, Mancs, people from all over the UK who were drawn to the bright lights of the borough. The South Africans in Earls Court were selling Durban Poison - Durban Poison is a Sativa strain that originates from the beautiful sunny port city of Durban in South Africa, a real nice smoke that could blow your head off - along with the gays in Earls Court, who were selling MDMA, commonly known as ecstasy, a psychoactive drug primarily used for recreational purposes. The desired effects include altered sensations, increased energy, empathy, as well as pleasure. When taken by mouth, the effects begin in 30 to 45 minutes and last 3 to 6 hours.

Earls Court is a district in the Royal Borough of Kensington and Chelsea, in West London, bordering the rail tracks of the West London line and District line that separate it from the ancient borough of Fulham.

I had met an Irish guy called Phil who was a mechanic by day and dressed up as a woman by night. I didn't give a fuck, he did me no harm and he was funny, what he did in his spare time was no business of mine. I wasn't a narrow-minded homophobic for fuck's sake, this was a huge city where people didn't even bat an eyelid. He had a car and could be useful for lifts when I needed a driver. I had met Phil in one of the local pubs when he was

15

looking for weed. He introduced me to his mate Ginti, who lived in Shepherd's Bush and turned out to be a great friend over the years.

Most of the clubs and bars in the area were run by Jamaican and Moroccan doormen. They took no shit and could stand up to the gangs in the area who fought over their patches. The doormen knew me though; I caused no trouble and was up for a laugh, and they usually let me in free of charge. I never pretended to be something I wasn't, but when warranted I could blag and bullshit along with the best of them.

You get your cliques in any area: some people will like you, others don't. Since I was a kid I would go to places on my own: I didn't want an army of friends to go out with, one or two close friends who you could be open with was fine by me. People will talk shit about you anyway, the trick is not to take it personally. The book *The Four Agreements* by Don Miguel Ruiz that came out in 1997 taught me that. I don't care how much money or how much better educated you are, you're no better than me, and I'm no better than you.

Life is fleeting; enjoy the ride, don't be in awe of anybody. There are a lot of people out there who will rip you off or put you down, but that's always going to be the way. I moved in a lot of circles over the years and met loads of them. I also met good people who have turned out to be diamonds. You just must deal with them all, at some point in your lives. The older I get, I may not know what I want, but I know what I don't want.

On the whole, I am a loner and a free spirit. I like my own company at times. People will judge you by the clothes you wear and the job you have; I judge people on their sense of humour and how they make me laugh. I've had money, and I've been skint, but I never looked down on anybody. People have fallen out with me, or vice versa; I'm no angel, but that's life.

Of course, there is another side to Notting Hill, the wealthy, the big houses; I'm not writing about that so much, it's already been done in the film *Notting Hill*.

I had stayed off the booze for a few years, just drinking water and having the odd spliff or a tab of acid; it was too boring doing nothing whatsoever. I had figured people would take me more seriously if I wasn't tanked up all the time.

When I ended up booking the bands at the Mau Mau Bar on Portobello Road, a young lad called Matt Bicknell, the guitarist from a band called Stolen Colours, bought me sambuca at the end of the night, and I necked it, and that was me back on the booze; but to be honest, he did me a favour, as it was easier to connect with people when they saw you drinking. Thanks, Matt.

Living at Tony's was crazy at times. There were four or five lodgers and there were always parties going on and people were constantly coming and going. People scoring, having parties in their rooms, all the rogues of the area would turn up at some point, so I gradually got to know who was on the manor. I had a tiny box room on the top floor, but that suited me fine. I had a place to lay my head and lots of books to keep me occupied when I wasn't out and about.

Some of my fellow lodgers were running to Dubai, filling up a couple of suitcases full of cigarettes and bringing them back to London to sell on around the pubs and clubs of Notting Hill, another good earner. If they were caught, they would have the cigarettes confiscated, but usually they sailed through customs at Heathrow or Gatwick. Everybody was trying to make a shilling in one way or the other.

My mate from Warrington, Rob, who lived in the area, had sorted me out with Tony for the room when I got kicked out of the flat in Brixton, and he was always coming around. Rob was a painter and decorator and knew everybody in the area. He always found a job painting locally, he had the gift of the gab and was always up for a laugh. I had been living with him in his spare room at Markland House, near Latimer Road tube station, before I had been incarcerated in Jamaica.

We had known each other since we were about 11, back in Warrington. He loved northern soul and punk when he was a kid. When we were growing up back in Warrington he lived a few streets away from me. He was an only child and always had the best of everything; he was a snappy dresser, and usually had a gang of women hanging about around him. He was a good looking guy, with a shed load of charisma, and we had some great laughs over

17

the years; we fell out occasionally, he always spoke his mind, but we soon got over it, we were lifetime friends and had a lot of history between us.

He would always have my back if the shit hit the fan: that was his nature. All kinds of scallys would turn up from back in Warrington, coming to London on the mooch, and we would go to the 100 Club when they had the monthly northern soul nights and dance the night away. They were all good mates from back home, up for anything and game for a laugh.

'Life is what happens when you're busy making other plans'
- John Lennon

Market Traders

London's Portobello Road & Golborne Road market is probably the world's best-known street market, with a history stretching back over 150 years. The market is famous for its antique and bric-a-brac stalls and shops, but it also features a superb selection of fashion, food, crafts, books, and music. Hundreds of traders sell all sorts of everything, old and new, and there's plenty of delicious street food from all around the world.

On Fridays and Saturdays, the market stalls stretch a mile along Portobello Road and round the corner into Golborne Road. Sunday is another busy day and there are stalls and shops open every day of the week except Thursday afternoons, when shops are open but there are no stalls trading.

There was always somebody on the hustle around here and you soon got to know them when you were out and about. I ended up working on Portobello Road with a guy called Marcus, who had a room at Tony's, and a stall selling socks and underpants. It was a good earner for him because his customers were constantly buying from him: people always needed socks and underpants, much like toilet paper, you could never have too much. If you found a good niche on the stalls of Portobello you were a winner;

competition could be fierce. I enjoyed working on the markets and it brought me into contact with a lot of people, and people meant opportunities.

The market traders were a hardy bunch, out in all weathers, and they all kept their eye out for each other. Portobello Market had been trading for well over a century and the tourists would flock to it from all corners of London and indeed the planet.

Everybody was drinking in Finches, as it was called in those days, The Duke of Wellington, a meeting place for all the locals in the area, journalists, writers, musicians, market traders, football heads, construction workers, and tourists, all freely mingling in there together, and you would catch up on all the news about what was going on in the area. Built in 1854, and designed by Thomas Pocock, it was enlarged in 2001 when knocked through into the former shop next door, giving a two-room layout. Located on a corner of Portobello Road, this Young's pub is at the heart of the present-day market and attracts many visitors.

Waking up in Tony's house you never knew what was going to happen from one day to the next; it was like the hub of Portobello for comings and goings. I had just finished reading *The Ragged Trousered Philanthropists* by Robert Tressell, and it felt like we were still living in those days, the workers serving their betters, and Notting Hill was the perfect place to see the haves and the have nots all mingling together.

My life was spent living under the margins, and my wages were having fun at gigs with like-minded people. I loved this quote from George, 'having found people with money had no imagination and people without money had plenty of imagination.' Even so a man who was minted with the heart of a skinflint could give much more than a man who had fuck all.

One afternoon I heard a knock on my door. It was Tony looking for the rent. I got my wallet out and counted five £10 notes and handed it over, realising how lucky I was to be living in the house in such a great area and only paying £50 a week. Tony said, 'I'm cooking breakfast if you want any.' I was famished and followed him down the stairs to the communal kitchen and we ate, while Tony filled me in on the latest news that had been happening in his world. He always had a load of grafters working for him;

they would appear in the mornings and he would give them 10 wraps of sniff and whatever else they wanted. He never wrote anything down, he stored it all in his head, but he always knew to the penny who owed him what.

Tony was built like a little pit bull. Everybody knew him. He had gone to school at the local Holland Park, but got expelled. He was much smarter than the teachers at school, he knew it and they knew it. He was a born salesman and he set out on life with a keen entrepreneurial streak to make money and have fun at the same time.

He started to get me CDs and give them to me for when I was DJing at the Mau Mau Bar. He was making serious money, good luck to him, it could all come crashing down around him if he were collared. Tony lived by the motto 'you only live once.' I learned a lot through Tony; on the history of Notting Hill he was a mine of information, in all subjects.

When Notting Hill Carnival came around, all the locals were looking to make money, charging people to use their toilets, selling beers in dustbins filled with ice and Red Stripes, selling food. Sound systems would be set up outside houses, and it would be a great two-day party; drugs and weed would be plentiful and the most beautiful women would gravitate from all over the world for the greatest street party in Europe.

I used to love walking around on the Sunday morning when it was all starting up. It was the children's day and all the families would be out, and you could walk around quite safely and freely; all the sound systems would be blaring and the procession of lorries carrying the floats is a magnificent sight to clap your eyes on.

On the Monday, which was the main day, it would be rammed solid on the streets, and there would be pockets of trouble, but the sheer scale of the carnival is over a million people, so the trouble makers are a very tiny minority. Most of the people were there to have fun, which was right up my street.

People were having parties in their houses; it really is a fantastic experience, and if you have never been you should go at least once in your life. Don't be put off by the news stories they seem to churn out each year when it's over. When the carnival was over in the later years, the council would have the road sweepers out, and by the following evening it was like nothing had happened, the streets were so clean, and tons of rubbish had been moved.

I was always meeting new people, musicians who had moved into the area dreaming of stardom, but as the months and years rolled by you could see the bitterness in their eyes from years of rejections. Some turned to drugs to dull the pain of getting nowhere and feeling under-appreciated, and there was always a dealer lurking somewhere ready to solve their problems - 'Want a £10 bag mate?' - and then the cycle would begin, phone calls in the middle of the night, hours chasing up dealers and then back to their bedsits to play the guitar and dream again of hitting the big time, safe in the knowledge and cocooned by the warm glow of smack.

The sensible musicians would have a job on the side, working in the pubs or building sites scattered all over London. A city of nine million people could eat you up and leave you destitute if you weren't careful.

The older musicians were a different kettle of fish; they had given up on the dream of stardom years ago and would just play music for the sheer love of it, which looking back on it was the best reason of all.

Creative people are a totally different bunch of people. Some were constantly bubbling with ideas and came up with some fascinating insights into the ways of the world, and it was good to be around them when they were flowing with ideas and in good moods. Other times they could make your life hell if they were going through a bad patch and drinking heavily and doing far too many drugs, but in many ways, I was able to understand them, as I'd been there myself.

You could wander out of Notting Hill Gate tube station on a Saturday morning and amble along to the top of Portobello Road, making your way down the length of the Bella just over a mile, until you reached the Golborne Road. You would see all sorts of things, buskers banging out their songs, tourists buying off the stallholders, the pubs would be packed out, and the road would be teeming with life.

'I've never had problems with drugs. I've had problems with the police'
- Keith Richards

I had met the scouse - the Assassin was the street name he used - years before, through my mate Rob who used to score weed from him. He reminded me of a friend of mine who had been killed in a car crash years before, Ste Hardman; they had a similar kind of look. Assassin was small and wiry. He had a studio on Lancaster Road, and was obsessed with reggae and The New World Order. He was writing a book on it, 'I-Magi-Nation (The Divine Chess Game)', a magic, mystery, and manipulation conspiratorial study of the 'hidden paths that create our now global civilisation'. He was also a reggae-inspired music mixer and producer, about to release an album *Freedom is Dead – Long Live Freedom* with the project/band name Prisoners of Democracy. He became a Wing-Chun Kung-Fu adherent and martial arts teacher and had been in London for many years.

He told me as a young dude he didn't clean up his act until almost 30. 'I did everything wrong,' he said. 'I was damaged. I was a gang member, a fighter, a drug addict. At 29 I had to decide whether to die or live, and I started making music. I always wanted to do that and then I also discovered martial arts, and it all came together.' He began training in Wing-Chun Kung-Fu, in the Bruce Lee style. 'After spending years practising this style, I needed more data about how to generate power, so I found a guy living in West London who was a disciple of Mah-Li Yeung/Yang, and I became his student.

'I've mostly mixed and produced over the years and I'm probably the underground artists' underground artist. I was quite well known but it wasn't very commercial. My hero was Adrian Sherwood, a white reggae producer, his label was called On-U-Sound. His artist stable also included Ari Up from The Slits and Mark Stewart and the Mafia. Sherwood was crazy, a living genius, and very, very heavy!'

Assassin also got a break from Mohamed Al-Fayed's son-in-law Noah Francis Johnson, a former trainee priest, Welsh boxing star, world disco dancing champion, and heavy metal rocker. 'Noah Francis was brought to my house because he was doing a rework of a track that was first done by Tapper Zukie, and he wanted a reggae sound. He asked me a lot of questions about my concepts and ideas and I met his wife, Jasmine Al-Fayed.' I found Assassin to be quite out there with his thoughts, but we got along, and he would sometimes come and play a gig for me.

He was also sitting on hundreds of kilos of the best hash in Europe; you would never tell, he walked around as if he didn't have two pennies to rub together, he was very quiet and never bragged about anything. He was well connected in Liverpool and van loads of hash went through him and his studios on a weekly basis, ready to be dispersed around London and beyond. He kept his mouth well and truly shut and operated in virtual anonymity for years.

I met Matthew Snell around 2004. He was always out and about chatting to all the good-looking women in the bar, gregarious and well-spoken. He lived on Lancaster Road with his mother Jacqui. Matt was disabled, but that never stopped him doing anything and he never complained. His father had produced the cult film *The Wicker Man* in 1973 and lived in Los Angeles. Matt was always having parties around at his house, and there were always beautiful women there; he knew how to entertain and was a fantastic host. He was always full of ideas, and for fun, he started booking bands with me at various venues. We did a series of gigs and had a whale of a time, happy days.

I decided to try and locate Mentona K, the singer I had been working with in Thailand, who had been missing for over four years now. I had invested a lot of time and money in him, and I really was curious to find out what may have befallen him. I went along to the Liberian Embassy and met the Consulate; his name was Geoff Dowana. I explained the situation, and he said he would investigate it. I gave him all the details and a few weeks later he gave me a call to come and see him.

I was hoping that they had finally located him. When I got there, he explained that he had not made contact, but he suggested that I should contact his friend in Liberia who ran a newspaper over there. I was disappointed, but thanked him profusely; he laughed and said no bother.

I cast my mind back and thought of all the escapades that had happened in the last 4 years, and I felt finding him was almost like looking for a clean needle in a junkie's backyard.

That night I set about sending an email.

Dear Willem,

I have recently spoken with Mr. Dowanna of the Liberian Embassy in London; he has said it is okay to contact him by email. If you need more information regarding Gregory John Karkor, it will be a splendid idea to put his name and the details of his missing person on page 11 of your newspaper. We must also think of other ways to make contact for his whereabouts, this is especially important we locate him, we have grave fears for his safety. When you need more information from me please contact me at once.

A few days later Willem replied that he would put the word out.

Dear Willem,
Thanks ever so much for making contact.

I gave him further details: Gregory John Karkor Passport No or/0018668-98 issued in Monrovia 15 December 1998 expires 14 December 2008. Mr. Mentona had been living in Thailand for nine months; when I last heard from him, he was supposed to come to the UK for promotional work. Everything was fine up to until around 4 years ago when all contact was lost. I had grave concerns for his safety and feared he might be in some Bangkok hellhole or worse.

Mentona K is a Liberian artist. Born in a third world country, Liberia, on the West Coast of Africa, Mentona spent most of his early years singing songs for his family and their friends. Liberia was one of the first countries in Africa to be recognised as an independent state on July 26th, 1847. It is now host to three and a half million citizens. However, all was not peaceful in Mentona's homeland in the past years (1990-1997) as it was ravished with war and civil unrest. Mentona himself was forced to flee to the Ivory Coast. 'Mentona' is an African word which means boy who grows to be a man quickly, and this boy certainly did. Born on the 24th of July 1977, he had been singing and writing songs since he was ten years old and had been inspired by great singers such as Bob Marley and Jimmy Cliff. And Mentona too will aspire to such heights.

Liberia, officially the Republic of Liberia, is on the West African coast. It is bordered by Sierra Leone to its northwest, Guinea to its north, Ivory Coast to its east, and the Atlantic Ocean to its south-southwest. The country's capital and largest city is Monrovia.

Well, I had done my bit; I never really held out much hope that I would find him. I've scoured the Internet but to no avail, so far.

Karma

I used to go and visit my sister in Fareham, to get out of London now and then, for a break. Fareham is a market town at the north-west tip of Portsmouth harbour, between the cities of Portsmouth and Southampton in south east Hampshire. It gives its name to the Borough of Fareham. It was historically an important manufacturer of bricks, used to build the Royal Albert Hall.

I had spent 18 months living in Portsmouth, years before. I loved Southsea where I had lived with my brother and my cousin Darren and my girlfriend at the time, Jo. It had been a good time; Portsmouth was full of characters. We always had a good time there; I have lots of family in the area. I had mates who had the keys for the old red phone boxes and they would go round at nights into the phone boxes and unlock the cash boxes and empty them and lock them back up. One of my mates found a gun in there one day; God knows what a gun was doing in one of the cash boxes. He took it though, as a souvenir.

There are so many scams going on all over the country that we are never even aware of.

Back in the days when we had been 'ringing in the changes', it had been our base for a while. We roamed the rest of the country like bandits. I'm glad I gave it up in the end: easy money is never easy, there is always a price to pay in the end. The scam was one in which we would con shop cashiers out of money who worked the tills all over the country, Europe, and places throughout the world. We would go and chance our luck.

It can work in many ways but usually involves swapping notes for other notes or coins, then back again.

We would buy something small with a £20 note, for example, something which costs 20p or under a pound. The cashier hands back the change, a £10 note, a £5 note, four pound coins, and 80p in silver. Then I would say 'Sorry, I have enough coins in change, I've just found them in my other pocket.' This works because most of the cashiers were glad to get the change back because they always wanted change throughout their shift that day. I would slip the £10 note into my back pocket, and in my hand I would have £5 note and the coins, to make it up to £10, and ask for a £10 note back, then point my hand to the till, so I had £5, four £1 coins and the shrapnel. 9 times out of 10 they would go back to the till and get the £10. I would reach over and take the £10 note out of their hand, and then count out the change back to the shopkeeper, and put the fiver in their hand all the time talking to them 5, 6, 7, 8, 9, and then I would put the £10 pound note back in their hand on top of the money I had already placed in their hand they have just given me, making £19 in their hand, and throw the rest of the shrapnel on top of the money in their hand. I would say, I tell you what I will just have the £20 note back and point at the till again with my hand, they would see in their hand a £10 note a £5 note and £5 in coins making £20.

They would count it again and see £20; you could see it in their head, see it ticking over on their face, yes this is all correct. Then they would go back to the till and give you the £20 back, whereas in reality, you had made £30, the £10 you had in your back pocket, and the original £20; it was such a simple scam and nobody was any the wiser.

Sometimes you could be cheeky and take the £20 note off them and slip that in your back pocket as well. Then you would keep talking to the cashier and ask for a box of matches; they would come back and you would give them some coins and when you had paid, you would just stand there and they would look at you, and you would say can I have the £20 note back with a smile on your face like you could be trusted. Usually, they would then say, oh sorry, I never gave it to you, and go back to the till and hand you another £20, so now, in reality, you had your original £20, plus another £20 plus £10, so you had made £30. We would call that a double up.

If you really wanted to go for it again, you would buy another box of cheap biscuits or whatever and then pay again, and do the same, just stand there and they would look at you again and ask if everything was OK? Then you would say, oh, just waiting for the £20 back, then if they fell for it they would go back and give you another £20 back. We would call that a treble up.

You had scammed them three times on the trot, so you had your original £20, and made £10, then £20, then another £20 so you had just made £50 cash plus your twenty back, so you now had £70. It was like they were under your spell and were hypnotised to follow out your orders without realising what was going on. Walking away chatting, saying have a nice day, leaving them with a bewildered look on their face, we would walk straight out, and go in the shop next door and do the same, and then into the next shop, and carry on till you run out of shops.

We would jump in the car and go to the next town and carry on doing it, sometimes doing every till in one supermarket; there was nobody we didn't do, taxi drivers, carpet shops, ice cream vans. In the evenings we would do pubs, chip shops, off-licences, anybody who had a till was fair game. It took me around the world to many countries. There was nowhere we wouldn't go, in any denomination; there are hundreds of variations and different ways of doing it with a £50 note or 100 notes in whichever country you were in. On a typical day we would go out in the car, usually working in pairs, and would head out all over the country, any city any village any town, we would turn up at some point; sometimes we would do a week trip, even going to Ireland and slipping across the border into Northern Ireland after taking the ferry across from Holyhead to do a two-week trip, bang at it seven days a week.

I remember in Australia doing 8 or 10-week trips, every single day grafting; it was like being a travelling salesman constantly on the road, relentlessly doing every shop we could find.

Going back over the same routes every couple of months, sometimes you would do the same shopkeeper 10 times over a year. They still would not twig it; we really did take the piss, sometimes doing the same shopkeeper twice in the same day, and they would say with a smile on their face, 'Oh somebody did that to me this morning', still none the wiser.

Occasionally somebody would twig it, but then I would blag my way out of it, act daft and say sorry, but not very often. It was truly a trick that is so easy. Even if you describe it to someone they find it really hard to get it, and most people couldn't be bothered doing it, thinking all that trouble for a tenner, scratch their heads and wonder why.

We would be raking in thousands each week. Some of us had serious drug problems, and you could easily become paranoid after years and years of doing it. I gave it up in 1998: I got a conscience, I just realised the karma of it all. And I truly am sorry for all the aggravation and hassle I gave people over the years, it was fraud and deception and probably lost some of the staff their jobs, and I truly wonder why I carried on for all those years. This is part of the reason I have tried over the years to do the right thing and help people. I've made some serious fuck-ups in my life, and I do regret the hurt I've caused people, and the hurt I've brought down on myself, what a tosser I had been.

People are still doing it nationwide; it becomes a way of life, an addictive way of earning a living to survive. It will stop when all transactions are done by a plastic card, but the scammers will move on and find another scam somewhere.

I was taking so many drugs around this time while we were living in Southsea. My Irish mate brought a load of coke back in the 90s from the States; he was being paid to mule it through, but he did a runner and fucked off with all the gear, without handing any over to his contact. He started dishing it out dirt cheap, bringing it to me. We went on a crack bender for months and started rocking it up in the flat, passing it on to some dude who ripped me off, which was probably a good move. We had to skip town in the end and fuck off to Asia. I was down to about 11 stone and developing a serious paranoid head; we had to get away before we all ended up in jail or a nuthouse.

Aw well, thank God them days are behind me and we lived to tell the tale. I spent a few more days with my sister Lynn and the family and then headed back to London in search of the next adventure.

'To have been a criminal is no disgrace. To remain one is a disgrace.'

- Malcolm X

Chapter Two

Back in London, Tony told me he was going to Chelsea in the morning. Chelsea is an area of south west London, bounded to the south by the River Thames. Its river frontage runs from Chelsea Bridge along the Chelsea Embankment, Cheyne Walk, Lots Road, and Chelsea Harbour. He would tell me the story when he got back; he was always up to something and his stories always amused me. A couple of hours later he came back and told me what had happened. I always wondered why he told me, but I think he trusted me and wanted somebody to unload the story on, and more importantly, he trusted me and wanted me to earn some cash.

He had been dealing with a rich guy who had offered good money for somebody to take hash to Luton. We spent hours chatting about it, and he asked me if I would do the run and take it there, and in the end, I said I would do it. He would give me £400. Fuck, here we go again, where my head was, I will never know. I always seemed to fall back on weed when I was in need: the money would come in handy. 'Money's too tight to mention' was going around in my head. Music and drugs went hand in hand, there was no doubt about that, and a man must do what he must do to survive in this life.

The following afternoon I arrived at St Pancras. I knew it was a massive gamble as I boarded the train to Luton: in my luggage was five kilos of Nepalese hash. If the police stopped me at the other end I was in the shit and would be looking at an automatic jail sentence if I got collared.

I settled back into my seat as the train took out of the station heading north. I just had to hold my nerve and hope for the best. Luton is about 30 miles outside of London, so we soon arrived there. The Nepalese kilos were well packed and hidden in the bottom of my holdall, so I should have no problems. So far so good, but it wasn't over yet. I made my way to meet the contact, big John I was told, who would be in a boozer not far from the station. I had his number but thought I would go to the pub first: I had a description and was sure I would suss him out.

I found the pub and went and ordered a pint off the girl behind the bar. It was quite busy with the office workers on their lunch. Somebody tapped me on the shoulder, and I turned around. It was John. He said to follow him, and we sat down at a table, away from the busy crowd.

John was around 18 stone, with long black hair, about 6ft 3in: he stood out in a crowd. He was wearing a green shirt and a pair of tracksuit bottoms, and looked like a wrestler with huge arms. He spoke with a Glaswegian accent.

'You brought the gear then?' he said.

'Yes, it's in the bag.'

Nepalese Hash takes one step above any other Nepalese region made hashish. Always known for super high-quality sticky black Nepalese hashish, it gets you extremely high. The concentration of THC is astounding. This hashish is not usually pressed with a machine, but hand-pressed, leaving behind a beautiful soft flexible texture. Some will argue their best to make sure you know the good super hash comes from Nepal. Simply by taking a close look, a well-seasoned veteran can tell the potency is superb. Touching certainly lets the user know this is good flexible THC glands stuck together.

John looked at the bag. I took a small piece out of my pocket, a tester I had, and gave it to him. He gave it a quick rub between his fingers under the table, and it melted between his fingertips. He grinned. 'Wow, this is great shit; you had no problems then?'

'No, everything went to plan.' He handed me the money in four white envelopes. I excused myself and went to the toilets, and in one of the cubicles I opened up the envelopes, and counted out the money to check it was all there; yes, it was all in £50 notes. I went back to the table with John. He said, 'This is chicken feed compared to what you can earn. I got so many customers crying out for cocaine; you could make some serious money if you brought it here next time.'

'Thanks, but no thanks, I'm not interested. I was just doing somebody a favour.'

'Fair enough,' he said.

John had a couple more beers and then he made his exit with the bag, to chase up his contacts to shift the gear. I started to get myself motivated and head back to London. I put the money in my side pocket and walked back to the train station.

I saw Tony later that day. He counted out the money, gave me back £400, and I left him to it.

A few weeks later Tony asked if I was game to go back to Luton again and make a few deliveries.

'Not, if it's Charlie, Tony,' I quickly answered.

'Okay,' he said.

I went to bed that night and thought it over, but no, I would stick with the music. I would rather be skint than start selling coke. I had pushed my luck with the last trip to Jamaica, enough was enough.

'I remember the first time I had sex; I kept the receipt'
- Groucho Marx

Repenting My Sins

Soho is an area of the City of Westminster, part of the West End of London. Originally a fashionable district for the aristocracy, it has been one of the main entertainment districts in the capital since the 19th century.

Some people, when you meet them, you should just say 'Fuck off.' I had met a few of them in my life. Everybody has a dark side, but some of them can exploit it to the maximum; if you're gullible there is always somebody out there who will befriend you and take advantage without a second thought.

Hookers roaming the streets of Soho full of smack, willing to fuck anybody to get the money for the next fix. Who gave a fuck if she had aids or herpes, 'Get your cock out and stick it in me, then give me my money, you stupid sad fuck'? Fisting punters upstairs in some cheap tacky room with yellow faded photos of women with no clothes on, sticking their fist up some dude's ass and giving it a twist for good measure, whilst with the other hand eating chips and gravy out of a polystyrene carton, and wondering what time the dealer was going to show up. Just another day in the office.

There is definitely a seedy side, killers on the run from across the globe, who turn up and make this city their home, go about their business and nobody none the wiser, unless you woke up with one of them, and found you were tied up, your mouth gagged, and screams of terror erupting from your mouth that nobody could hear. It may make a few lines in one of the papers if you were lucky.

Some of the homeless drinking special brew or methylated spirits to keep them warm and in good spirits, snarling and shouting at you to give them a couple of quid as you pass by. You were just another mug punter who they preyed on in the hope that you would throw them a few coins to get a few more cans or a line of brown.

These things go on all the time if you move in the wrong circles: drugs and violence most people are completely heedless to. Teenage boys giving out blow jobs to tourists who get lost on the back streets of Soho, pretending they weren't enjoying it because they had their wife at home waiting for them, 'Aw fuck it, suck harder you motherfucker, this has got to last me for a while', whilst their eyes were glazing over, just about to empty their seed in this teenage delinquent with rotting teeth who was gagging with impatience, waiting to move on to the next client.

The streets are littered with lost souls and rejects, and it could happen to anybody if you aren't careful. Go on, have another line, haemorrhage your bank account, fuck work, go on the game, start robbing punters, maybe even rob your friends and family. The devil talking to your dark side.

The streets aren't paved with gold, they are lined with the homeless fighting over spaces to lay their weary heads. They all have stories to tell of how they descended into the depths of society and couldn't sink any lower, unless of course they found themselves in a body bag, with the paramedic tutting how much effort they have to take to get you into the van, and transport you off to the local mortuary, nobody caring one bit. There to be dispatched off to one of the nearby cemeteries a few days later, buried by the state, nobody to mourn your loss because nobody knew who you were, and nobody cared anyway, just one less beggar on the streets of London.

How many of them I met; you would have to be blind not to see it. It could be me or you if fate fell the wrong way.

People come from all over to work the streets of Soho; money could be made. Old guys walking into the porn shops, looking to get their arse spanked by some obliging junkie whore, who would steal their wallet when their trousers lay on the bed, while they were in the throes of ecstasy, 'Spank me harder, harder,' they would be groaning, unaware the brass had just relieved them of their wallet. Tourists standing outside the sex shops egging each other on to go in and sample the delights inside, looking for some fun, full of drink and bravado. Heading home in the morning with hangovers, ashamed of what they had done the night before.

I heard all the tales. Two girls who came from Glasgow started scoring weed off me. They were making good money earning up to £5,000 a week and took long holidays; they were the type who had their heads screwed on and had nice gaffs in Maida Vale, it was just a job for them.

Soho is being cleaned up more and more these days and the criminals are moving east, chasing money and dreams of stardom elsewhere.

'Don't take life too seriously, you can't get out alive anyhow'
                                              - Hank Williams

Bayswater is an area within the City of Westminster and the Royal Borough of Kensington and Chelsea in West London. It is a built-up district located 2.5 miles (4.0 km) west-northwest of Charing Cross, bordering the north of Kensington Gardens. Bayswater is one of London's most cosmopolitan areas: a diverse local population is augmented by a high concentration of hotels. In addition to English, there are many other nationalities. Notable ethnic groups include Greeks, French, Americans, Brazilians, Italians, Irish, Arabs, and many others.

I hooked up with my old friend Dandi, London-Irish, his family hailing from Dublin. He had been living in Bayswater for over 25 years. He was a great laugh; he would recite Shakespeare and he had been in the band I was managing, NRG Fly, before I got nicked in Jamaica. They had split up after too many drug problems. The guitarist Dave went to rehab, the singer Andy carried on smoking crack, and that was that. We talked about the old days at his flat and how things had been going since my absence. I left him later that day and walked home back to Portobello Road.

I knew so many people in the community. It's a great vibe around Portobello. I had lots of friends, JC001 the rapper was born around there, Bubbles and Ronnie were great characters, Kenny Fearon my scouse mate and Geordie Jimmy; lots of Jamaican friends, Daddy Vego on All Saints Road, a legend in the music business and had a shop, People Sound. KJ was always in the Mau Mau Bar, dressed sharp and had a good laugh, and Brains who had come from Jamaica when he was 19, a good man.

I put a night on at the Mau Mau Bar. I knew the then owner, Swan from Croatia. I started DJing there on a Saturday and booking the acts for a couple of years. I put the Alabama 3 on in the Mau Mau Bar a few times; Larry Love on vocals, Mark Sams on guitar, Nick Reynolds on harmonica. Nick was the son of the great train robber Bruce Richard Reynolds; they were a great bunch of characters who had met in rehab. Their big hit at the time was 'Woke Up This Morning', which was the theme tune for the gangster program *The Sopranos*. A great band who deserve more.

I met Howard Marks a few times in Notting Hill and we chatted about doing the fundraiser for the charity Prisoners Abroad based in Finsbury Park. Howard was a terribly busy man.

I was also working on the stalls on Portobello a few days a week selling socks and undies, with my mate Marcus.

I was out every night spotting bands. I was always in the Notting Hill Arts Club, run by Scotsman Alan McGee who put Primal Scream and Oasis on the map. He had the Wednesday nights rocking in there. I met Liam Gallagher down there many times, and we chatted. He knew my cousin Jack, through Noel. We had a laugh; I was a northerner and I think he liked that; he kissed my hand. I like Liam, he's a nice guy.

I met Kate Moss too, and had a little dance with her. Just a laugh down there, Bobby from the Primal's, all kinds of celebrities were going in there. They weren't my mates, but I met them on numerous occasions.

Everybody hung out around Notting Hill. You would see all kinds of stars. I wasn't fazed, they're just people. I worked for a while for Stage Miracles as a production runner. The wages were crap, but I got to work on all the big major venues. I worked with and met Madonna, U2, The Darkness, and loads of others. I used to see Ian Brown a lot from the Stone Roses, and rehearsed with them once, playing my bongos at the Inn on the Green. Ian was rehearsing for some show for the magician Dynamo. Ian was originally from Warrington, like me, and moved to Manchester when he was six. We got along, and he took me for a Malaysian on Portobello Road. We had a laugh. I like Ian; people are people, good, bad, and indifferent.

Portobello has a history of music; Hawkwind, The Clash, The Pink Fairies all cut their teeth in the venues around the Grove. Bob Marley recorded Exodus at Sarm Studios. I used to see Seal and even spotted Robert De Niro once. My mate Bob Tydor taught Madonna guitar; she had a house around there.

I enjoyed living on Westbourne Park Road and was quite happily settling back into the groove. Life was sweet. I did a DJ spot at Filthy McNasty's in Angel where I met Steve 'Fatty Molloy'; he won Roadie of the Year working with Primal Scream, what a party that was! My mate Rob turned up with loads of Es. The place was packed to the rafters. Shane McGowan from the Pogues, it was his pub. I met a girl from Columbia called Rosa that night and at some point we slipped back to her flat in Angel, where she pulled out a massive rock of pure Charlie.

Okay, I was off again. Here was this stunning girl, about 35; she put some Rolling Stones on, and we partied for the rest of the night. She wasn't looking for a boyfriend, she already had one, and he was due back in a few days from Columbia. I made up for the time back in Jamaica; she gave me a good time and that was an understatement.

I left her house a couple of days later and jumped a cab back to Westbourne Park Road. I slipped into bed with a smile on my face and slept for about 24 hours straight. I was shattered.

I was all over London: West, East, South, North. I went to loads of gigs and squat parties. Sometimes it was like being in the bowels of hell in some of the squats, weirdos full of ketamine. I loved it the wilder and stranger it was: I buzz on weird atmospheres. I started to meet everybody on the music scene, from the underground bands at least. I went out every night, and it just went by in a blur; I was making up for the lost time. What a life: here I was, I had virtually turned myself into a slave, trying to help musicians, and forgot about my own life. Everything was put on hold, I was at everybody's beck and call, but this was the life I had chosen.

My life of petty crime was still going on; would I ever learn? Still, I discovered things about myself. I would have been lost in some dead-end job, I liked taking risks and challenging myself constantly, so I just had to get on with it and hope for the best. Everywhere I went I was constantly surrounded by drug dealers in the various pubs and clubs I was frequenting. The lure of easy money was hard to resist, and I carried on with blind faith that my luck would change in the music business.

People came and went constantly in my life, things changed, people moved on. It wasn't all gloom and doom though; I was having the time of my life. Anything beat being back in that rat-infested hell hole in Jamaica, I would remind myself when things weren't going too well.

I'd been a wild and reckless youth and not much had changed. I think that was the reason I got on with the younger musicians. I wasn't jaded with it all and like to think they respected me for that. I may not have had loads of money, but if I did, it wouldn't take them long to get it out of me. I had put my money where my mouth was quite a few times; aw fuck, life is a gamble, and so short, even the young ones will become old eventually. What else was I going to do, sit around watching *EastEnders*? Fuck that, life is for living. The day to day of life, with all its mundanity, was not appealing to me one bit.

Perhaps I could have stayed in my hometown, settled down with a steady job and lived a quiet life, but no, I had to go and seek adventure. If I go to my grave with nothing, I can at least say to myself I had a go, I went and looked around.

Although Albert Einstein said 'A calm and modest life brings more happiness than the pursuit of success combined with constant restlessness' it was far too late for me by now; or was it?

I met people from all walks of life and learned so much from them.

'A man is a success if he gets up in the morning and gets to bed at night, and in between does what he wants.'
- Bob Dylan

Inn on the Green

One day I got chatting with a guy who was selling records on Portobello Road. His name was Graham, a bit of a sarcastic fucker, but we got on. Through him, I met his mate, Denny. They both had an encyclopaedic knowledge of music; if one didn't know something about some obscure record, the other did.

We all got along, and we approached Dave and his wife Tina, the owners of the Inn on the Green, the music venue on Thorpe Close which used to be a snooker hall; we hit them with our plan, and they offered us six weeks of Friday nights to see what we could do to bring people there. So we arranged six-weeks-worth of gigs between us. Graham, Denny and I knew all the bands in the area, and we advertised on gumtree, and put posters in the music shops around Portobello Road.

Over the weeks we did some great gigs and the word started to spread. We printed up loads of flyers and posted them everywhere. I was standing on the street handing flyers out to passersby.

Denny was doing the sound and DJing, we had various girls taking the money on the doors and I was introducing the bands. Graham was a mine of information and loved music, and we built a great scene. We called the night One Flew Over The Cuckoo's Nest.

We were all completely different characters - but somehow it worked.

We finally arranged a gig with my old friend Howard Marks, setting the date for November 2005 at the Inn on the Green. We also booked Alabama 3 and the actor Ray Winston's daughter Lois who was in a band called Crack Village. The lead singer of Alabama's, Rob Spragg aka Larry Love, is Welsh - he and Howard Marks get on like brothers, being Welsh, kindred spirits!

We had the flyers printed up and blitzed the area with them:

Helping Prisoners Abroad

Venue: The Inn on The Green (3 Thorpe Close Ladbroke Grove W10 5XL) under the Westway and above Portobello fitness Club. Approx. 4 mins walk from Ladbroke Grove Tube.

Line Up: from South Wales Howard Marks, aka Mr. Nice, Alabama 3, Crack Village, Paddy Hill from the Miscarriage Of Justice Organisation.

MOJO the organisation was founded in 2001 by Paddy Joe Hill, one of six innocent men wrongfully convicted in 1975 for the Birmingham pub bombings. The Birmingham Six's convictions were finally quashed, and they were released in March 1991. Paddy made a pledge to campaign for those he had left behind, to bring a voice to the voiceless. At that time, he thought he might have to take a year out campaigning on their behalf, before trying to build a life for himself outside of prison. In any event, he has now been campaigning for over twenty-seven years.

Also on the bill that night was Rita Batecelli, Static Attack, DJs I-Shen & Django B. The flyer continued:

'Come on down and help make British prisoners' lives that little bit better. British prisoners who are rotting in jails all over the world need your help. Would you like to be involved in a memorable night? Then the Prisoners Abroad party is just for you. On your arrival you will be able to find out all you need to know, about the people who help.

'Howard Marks, who had spent seven years in prison in America, and then on his release wrote the bestselling book *Mr. Nice* will be doing his one-man show. The Alabama 3, who are the best live act in the country, will be giving their support. Crack Village, who are making great waves in the hip hop world, fronted by Lois Winstone. Toby Legend, talking on behalf of Prisoners Abroad on his experience in the General Penitentiary in Kingston, Jamaica. Toby's Motto - "Rock 'n' roll saves lives".'

The night of the gig it was rammed: over 400 people turned up. I joined Alabama 3 on stage playing the bongos. My mate Johnny Wood filmed it and my Polish friend, Peter Adamc, took the photos. Howard, with his one-man show, went down a storm.

We raised over £2000, with Denny doing the DJing, and all the money went to the charity Prisoners Abroad. I felt it was good for my karma. The Prisoners Abroad organisation had helped me out so much, and to be honest it's not easy to raise money for unsuccessful drug smugglers, but they do a fantastic job and it was a pleasure to give something back.

Prisoners Abroad was formed as the National Council for the Welfare of Prisoners Abroad in 1978 and registered as a charity on 24th April 1980.

Rock On Tommy

Over time Graham fell in love with a girl from Romania, who had been working on the door taking the money, and he eventually moved there with her. Denny and I ended up running the night for the next two years, and boy, did we have fun.

Meeting all the locals in the area, the Inn on the Green became the place to be. Mick Jones from the Clash put on six Fridays there with his Carbon Silicon nights. It was a great success, and we had helped to bring it to the attention of the promoters, and people started coming in their droves.

Around this time my mate Paul, who I had gone to school with, had bought a flat in Canary Wharf. He was a Project Manager and he had been offered a job out in Dubai; I was a bit gutted he would be leaving London in November 2005. He had always been around since the 80s when I first came to London. When the time came, we had a good piss up, and we went to a friend's wedding - Janice and Richard who lived over in Camden. We had a great crack and the next day he flew out to take up the position he had been offered. People were always coming and going in my life.

One of the street beggars who I got to know over the years used to sit outside BestBuy on Portobello Road with a cap on the floor for people to throw money into. We always used to have a good chat; his name was Martin, he had a good sense of humour and we would have in-depth chats about everything under the sun. Sometimes he would say, 'Can you fuck off Tommy', because I was fucking his business up; I never took it to heart, after all, it was putting people off from stopping and throwing a few coins in his cap. He was in his early 40s, and he'd had a major smack problem; most of the street guys had issues, but there for the grace of God go I.

One day I noticed he wasn't there, and I started to ask around. I found out he had died. I was shocked; he was well-liked in the area, he was missed. He had a girlfriend, and I bumped into her, and she told me the sad news; she had no money, and I decided to try and help. I went and saw Dave at the Inn on the Green again and told him I wanted to put a gig on in memory of a friend, and he agreed, so we went ahead and booked the night. We got loads of flyers printed up, and I went around and told all the street guys, and the word started to spread over the next few weeks. I told his girlfriend and she was made up that something would be going on in his memory. It was a small gesture on my part and I just hoped people would turn up because I also had to fill the bar. Dave didn't want an empty bar, especially as he wasn't charging me for the hire of the venue.

On the night loads of the street guys turned up asking me if I could get them a pint, and did I have 50p? Dave was giving me daggers: I had brought all the beggars together in one room and nobody was spending, but luckily some of the locals turned up, and

41

friends who knew Martin from years ago came and spent some cash behind the bar at least. One of them was a guy called Julian Rendell, who had been great friends with Martin.

Julian was a very bright guy, who had been brought up in Notting Hill but ended up living with the travellers for years. He became the gypsy liaison officer sorting disputes out between the councils and travellers. He told me some great stories and we became good friends from then onwards. The night went well, and we all had a good laugh reminiscing about Martin, and his family sent their thanks. He came from Southampton originally, I believe.

We raised £300. I gave some to the Salvation Army on Portobello Road the next day, and the rest to his girlfriend. Dave never took much money on the bar; oh well, everybody deserves a good send-off. I used to joke, you know you are doing well in the music business when the bands turn up and play at your funeral. A life without passion would drive me insane.

My friend Rainbow George has this theory that we all have our parts to play in this life, and when it's all over you go somewhere, and wherever that may be, you get to watch your whole life from the minute you are born, until the moment you die, on a video. After you've watched it you must go out and sell it. The thinking behind the whole thing is to make your life as interesting as possible so that somebody will possibly want to buy it. So, don't waste a moment of it, go out there and do your thing; life is way too short for anything else. Would you like to make a million pounds before you die, or go to your grave owing a million pounds? I know which I would prefer. I won't be worrying when I'm gone.

Death is a strange thing, we're all going to be the stars of that show one day at our own funeral. Only a fool would think of death constantly, but the grim reaper is hovering about somewhere in the background awaiting us all, and with that in mind, make mine a double.

I've been in some states in my life, through drink and drugs, and generally having a ball; someone once said to me, 'You know your problem, Tommy? You think every day is Christmas', which in a way I do, but I am mellowing out. I love excitement, and love life with a passion, living in the moment, taking each day as it comes. We're all different, thankfully.

I was putting on gigs anywhere we could find a stage, Westbourne Studios, Notting Hill Arts Club, The Paradise in Kensal Rise, Tesco's disco, a little dive bar that was run by some guys from Montenegro that used to stay open until 3am, the Portobello Star. I had so much energy, I was like a man possessed.

At one of the gigs, a lady came along and introduced herself. 'My name is the Duchess,' she said in a sultry foreign accent. I knew it was a name she had made up, for whatever reason. She was very striking looking, dressed all in black with short blonde hair and blue eyes, in her early 40s I guessed. She was laughing and drinking champagne. 'What can I do for you?' I asked to have a drink; she smiled and gave me a glass of champagne from the bottle she had. We got chatting, and she told me she was half Romanian and half Swedish and lived in South Kensington. I was busy running the gig, so I excused myself and went to introduce the bands. The club was packed and jumping.

The Duchess amused herself by chatting to everybody, and boy could she talk, as I started to find out during that night!

Johnny, my mate from the Midlands, was part of the crew; he was a genius with anything technical, he did the light shows and could build websites. Johnny was awestruck by the Duchess; she had a magnetic personality. Every time I saw her that night, she would pass another glass of champagne to me. By the end of the night she said, 'Let's go and party.' I was game for anything and agreed. Johnny came along when we got outside, and she pointed to a Mercedes and we all jumped in. 'This is my driver; he takes me everywhere.' Wow, great, I thought. The driver started the car up and she told him to go to the Troubadour in Earls Court. When we arrived the driver stayed in the car and waited outside.

Everybody seemed to know her. I found out she was highly creative and used to be a singer and she had many business interests in London, she told me that evening. She was really funny and always laughing. She kept nipping to the toilets and after a while, I sussed she was high on cocaine; she just couldn't stop talking, although she was funny, so we went along with it, laughing at her wisecracks. Suddenly she said, 'I have to go, my driver will take you home.' We went outside and we all got in the car; first, we dropped Johnny off in Kilburn, then she dropped me off back at Portobello. Before I got out of the car, she gave me a big kiss and laughed, 'See you again.' As they pulled away from the curb, I waved and watched the taillights disappear into the distance. Just another crazy night, I thought before I fell asleep that night. It happened all the time at gigs, you could have random nights with strangers, and perhaps never see them again.

'Love the life you live. Live the life you love'
- Robert Nesta Marley

Chapter Three

One morning while we were having breakfast in the communal kitchen, Tony asked me if I wanted to make some money. I guessed what was coming next.

He was well connected. Could sort me out with weed or hash. He told me to think it over, there was money to be made. I was skint yet again and I wanted the cash to carry on in the music business. I thought it over for a few days and finally relented. Tony laid me on a few ounces of weed and basically set me up in business. Over the next few months, I found my customers.

It was easy at the gigs. There was always someone looking for something. I carried weed on me or would nip backwards and forwards to my room and the cycle began. I was constantly answering the phone from then on, delivering here there and everywhere. I had got back on my feet and paid Tony back, and I had sworn I would not go back to the game, but finances had dictated my future. It was all well and good being skint, but not forever I told myself. I was only making a wage, but it helped me to carry on with the bands.

One night I got out of the taxi with an ounce of the finest Purple Haze, wrapped up in clingfilm and ready to deliver to the latest punter who had come my way that week, recommended by a mate, who said: 'She is a very wealthy socialite who loves weed and money is no concern, as long as the shit is top-notch.'

Super stimulating and thought-provoking, Purple Haze is both an excellent solo strain, and if you are sharing this strain with your partner, Purple Haze is one of the most effective aphrodisiac strains out there! Haze has a deliciously sweet blueberry aroma combined with sharper, spicier notes. Breaking open Purple Haze's cured, dried buds reveals a slightly dank and musty smell with a slight tinge of berry. I knew she would love this batch. I had no doubt about that.

I knocked on the door and was greeted by a woman of about fortyish, who was good looking, dressed in shorts and showing tanned legs. On her t-shirt was emblazoned in red letters, Who the Fuck are you. I introduced myself. 'Thanks for coming,' she drooled in that sarcastic West London way the well-educated and extremely sure of themselves had, when they knew you were doing their bidding. I knew she was going to haggle about the price, those rich fuckers always did.

I only dealt with the ones who had money. Years of supplying taught me who was worth bothering with and who wasn't. I could tell by the look of her place on the King's Road in Chelsea that she had lots of paperwork at her disposal; this wasn't some council flat on the World's End Estate. She went on to say I had come recommended by some of her friends in Notting Hill, and they said I could be trusted. I laughed and played along with her: 'Yes, likewise.' I then asked her name and she said 'Camilla, but you can call me Cammy,' then burst out laughing. Here we go, I thought, she is getting ready to barter with me, but fuck it - it was Friday night, this was my last delivery. She was definitely looking good, and she knew it, probably thought I was some soft fucker and she could squeeze a few quid out of the deal.

'Come in, I won't bite.'

I followed her through to the front room. The walls were adorned with paintings of battle scenes; one looked like the battle of Waterloo. I took a closer look, it was.

'Would you like a drink before we get down to business?' She turned around, without waiting for a reply, and went into the kitchen. Fuck, she looked good in those pink shorts, I had to admit to myself. It made a nice change from some of the usual customers I had dealt with lately.

She came back with a couple of glasses that had been frosted in the freezer and a couple of bottles of Peroni, and invited me to sit down next to her on the red couch with the classy looking coffee table in front. She set down the bottles and I reached over her for my glass and the bottle. I got a smell of her perfume; it was Jo Malone, one of my favourites. I didn't want to get ensnared in anything till the deal was over, I thought to myself. She looked me in the eyes and raised her glass. 'Cheers.' I took a drink and she immediately asked me to get the weed out, or, as she called it, the 'mood lifter.'

I pulled the packet out; it was spot on 28 grams of the best Purple Haze I had seen in months. It's a great feeling if you are going to sell weed; make sure it's the best you can get your hands on. She gave me the thumbs up when she smelt it.

I watched as she broke down the cannabis into her grinder. After a couple of minutes, she took out her papers and loaded and shaped the joint. She started to roll it. She pinched the paper between her fingertips and rolled it back and forth then started to pack the Haze down into its final shape. She knew how to make a decent joint, and I was quite fascinated watching her do it: she had it down to a perfect art form.

She put the spliff into her mouth, took it out and said 'Have you got a light?' Taking out my lighter I lit her up. She took a few tokes, placed the spliff in the ashtray, got up and said 'Have some yourself.' I thought why not? I had a few tokes, wow this was good, the music was playing in the background and it felt like it went louder; I was buzzing off the Haze and all felt good in the world. We ended up passing the joint back and forth. I was really stoned, and we were chatting like we had known each other for years.

'I must get your money for you.' She went over to one of the drawers in the front room and came back with an envelope with brand new £20 notes. 'Two hundred I believe,' she murmured in such a sexy way that she took me off guard for a second. Then I snapped back into business mode.

'You're taking the piss, you know it's £220.'

'Oh, Penny told me it was £200.'

'Fuck what Penny said, she knows it's £220, otherwise I will take it back.'

She laughed. 'Ok, big boy, calm down.' She pulled out another £20 note, from the back pocket of her shorts. 'I must have forgotten, but who can blame me for trying?'

We both burst out laughing. I fancied her, and I liked her attitude.

47

I was from another world to her, but I could feel the chemistry between us. She said 'Let's go to the off-licence and get some more beers.' Yes, I thought, buzzing with anticipation. We went out to the local off-licence and I bought a case of beer; she bought a couple of bottles of Jack Daniels and we headed straight back to her gaff. Camilla switched up the music. We settled back on to the couch. She turned up the music even louder and started dancing around me in the room. Bending down, our lips locked, and she stuck her tongue in my mouth. She was a fast mover and I was slightly shocked. I grabbed her, and pulled her down on top of me.

Afterward, we never spoke a word for another 20 minutes. We just lay there. When we both came around, starting to come back to reality, she whispered in my ear, 'Fuck I am so stoned.' I knew what she meant; so was I.

She got up and made her way to the bathroom. 'I am going to take a quick shower.' She came back 10 minutes later looking refreshed, gave me a towel and winked 'Your turn now', pointing me in the direction of the shower. It was 3am in the morning, and I was wide awake. I took a cold shower and cleansed myself in her bathroom and wrapped a towel around myself. I went back to the room and immediately noticed she had changed into a nightdress. She looked like a she-devil as she turned the music up. Primal Scream's 'Rocks' was playing in the background. My eyes were all over her. I loved that accent of hers. It reminded me of the actress Helena Bonham Carter; that was a huge turn on.

It had been a few hard weeks previously to this evening. I was going to enjoy tonight. It looked like she was up for everything and anything, and she was stunning. I was under no illusions that she was using me, but hey, everybody uses everybody in this life, for one thing or another. Even if it was just a conversation.

I was in a deep sleep when I heard a loud knocking on the door coming from the front room. Fuck, my head was throbbing. Camilla threw a dressing gown on and went to answer the door, coming back a few minutes later. She passed me the money in the envelope from the night before, backed out of the door and put her finger to her lips 'shhh.' Quietly she closed the door behind her.

I heard voices. Then the front door closed. I wondered who it could have been.

Camilla came back. I had to leave: it was her boyfriend. She had sent him to go to the shop to get some bread and milk. I threw my clothes on, fucked off out the door as quick as I could, and headed back to Portobello Rd.

Keep On Keeping On

Camilla started coming to the gaff over the next few weeks. We would close the door; I wouldn't see anyone for days. We drifted apart after a while though. It had been good at the time. We both knew it would never last. There was too much going on around me. I was out to have an adventure.

I guessed that Tony was in some kind of relationship. He was a funny fucker, game for anything, always told me great stories, which I loved. He was up to all kinds; he was a money-making machine, no doubt about that. He had some great pills, and the bell was always going day and night - till Tony put a stop to it, in case the police started to take notice.

There were a lot of police informers in the area. They would grass you up to the coppers in the police station at the top of Notting Hill when they wanted to garner favour and collect some cash for dropping some poor fucker in the shit. Plainclothes drug squad would frequent the pubs and clubs in the area. You could always spot them, drinking alone, nursing a coke or half a lager. Watching everybody in that sneaky way the police have a habit of doing. It never really bothered me, but it paid to be aware of them. I left them alone and they stayed away from me.

Every now and then a street dealer would get busted. So it looked like the police were doing their duty. You knew when someone got nicked or had their door put through; it was the gossip for the next few days. Somebody had been banged up in Wormwood scrubs, the local jail, just up the road on Ducane Road.

You would hear about the stabbings that went on between the rival gangs. Mainly young kids off the estates, over some drug deal that had gone wrong. Money was owed, and some poor fucker would lose their life.

The Road To Nowhere

The Duchess kept appearing at the gigs over the next few months. I started to get to know her properly. She was doing so much coke it was hard not to find out. Around 1am she would always disappear and jump into the Mercedes waiting outside. I would say 'Where are you going?' She would say 'I have to work, darling,' laughing as she left.

One night she told me the full story. She had been communicating with around 300 guys around the world from her home in Romania. Pretending to be in love with them. Building up relationships; God, I thought, where would you get the time for all that? Would tell each one of them to send her money on the pretence she was going to meet them on a certain date in their home cities. Never took a lot of money, just enough for a return first-class ticket from Romania. Sat back and watched her bank account swell to well over £100,000 when the money finally stopped arriving. Hopped on to a flight to London, looking around for a business opportunity. Within weeks, she met an old Russian guy who ran an escort agency by telephone, directing hookers to hotels all around the city. He had a massive database of clients, and he was looking to retire; she offered him £50,000 to take over, he accepted the offer, and bingo, she was in business.

From then on, her nights were spent on the telephone directing customers, 1am till 6am her busiest time. She always disappeared in the night with her driver taking her back home so she could man the phones. She was on a good earner, taking a commission off all the girls. To be honest, I went back to her flat now and then, but it became boring. The phone was always going, and I would be left sitting on my own most of the night.

She was a wild woman, but we got on; she did make me laugh. We moved apart though. She started to drive me crazy. Her coke habit was becoming too much; the non-stop chatter became irritating, to say the least.

'There's no happy ending with cocaine, you either die, or go to jail, or else you run out'

- Sam Kinison

I was starving. I couldn't be arsed cooking anything and made my way out of the door and walked up Portobello Road, bumping into a few faces along the way that I knew. I had a chat with the Polish guy, Peter, who was out walking his dog: 'Hello Tommy, freezing today.' 'Yeah,' I replied. 'Give my regards to your sons.' I carried on to the greasy spoon on the top of the Bella. The wind was freezing today; the cafe was packed with builders on their dinner hour. I ordered a full English and sat down to await my order. The couple running the cafe were hard-working from Turkey, and they did a great fry up. I had been coming here for years and they knew me well; there really was a great community vibe in the area and I couldn't imagine living anywhere else in London. West is best.

My phone started ringing. It was Jimmy, in Belsize Park. Jimmy was a bike courier delivering parcels all over London, one of the best grafters in the city, he could sell anything to anyone; he was a cheeky cunt who loved the sound of his own voice, but we were friends. 'Are you coming for a beer?'

'Just the one,' I replied. I knew what he was like when he was pissed: he could start an argument in an empty house.

I finished my breakfast, paid the bill, and threw my coat on, making my way to the tube station. I jumped the tube to Belsize Park in north London, and headed to the Steeles, his local pub, down the road. He was waiting for me when I got there. He ordered a couple of beers. I had four ounces of Nepalese in my pocket. We sat down at the table. I told him the quality was really good; he laughed and said 'I only deal in kilos, show me.' I passed them to him under the table. He looked. He could tell the quality was mint, and he said 'Go on then, I'll do you a favour and take them for my personal.' I said '£900', he said 'Fuck off I'll give you £800', we haggled and eventually we settled on £850. I was glad to get rid of them, I wasn't Mr. Big; he thought he was though. We had a few more beers.

He knew everyone in the pub, and if he didn't know them, he would strike up a conversation and soon get to know them. After my beer, I left him chatting to some Irish girl that he had struck up a conversation with. I left them engrossed in each other, oblivious to me. I flagged a black cab and made my way back to west London, passing Regents Park and heading on home.

Murder in Portobello

I got to know a lot of the stallholders over the years. I used to go to one of the food stalls quite a lot, for decent Thai food: Mrs. Tasty, run by a Thai lady, who was married and had three children. The food was great. We used to laugh and joke in broken Thai to each other. Her name was Chamlong Allen, and she had been living in London for the past 15 years. She had set the business up with her husband, Irvin Allen.

You can imagine my shock when I heard she had been murdered in April 2005. She'd been found dead in a lock-up garage in Lonsdale Mews in Notting Hill of multiple stab wounds. All the stallholders who knew her were devastated. She had been a lovely woman. Everybody was talking about the murder and wondering who did it.

A few days later I heard her husband had been arrested for the murder. Irvin Allen had been a successful actor, playing the part of evil henchman, Che Che, and fought with short-lived George Lazenby in a Bond film. He'd also acted with Roger Moore in *The Saint*, and made appearances in the classic TV show *Z Cars*. He was in his late 60s. I used to see him walking around with his walking frame.

I decided to help the daughters to raise money towards the funeral expenses; you can only wonder how the children were coping with this, their mother had been murdered, and now their father had been charged with the murder.

I booked a night at the Mau Mau Bar a few weeks later. All the local musicians rallied around and the stallholders put the word out. All of her children were under 18, but two of them came along. The place was packed and we raised quite a lot of money which I gave to the girls to help out with funeral expenses, it was a small gesture but we all felt good that we had been able to help in some kind of way. The community is really something special in the area.

Life returned back to normal over the coming months. Her husband stood in the dock at the Old Bailey in February 2006, and it turned out they had been having marital problems a few months before she died. She had written in her diary that he wanted £100,000 from her for the stall. She said she had fled the house one night because she was scared he would hurt her.

After all the evidence was read out in court, Irvin was found not guilty of her murder, on the 15th of February 2006. His lawyer Sucheta Sarkis read a statement from the retired actor and former boxer saying 'I am thankful that this terrible ordeal is over and I am found not guilty of the sad death of my wife. My thoughts at this moment are with my children that have stood with me throughout the long months that have taken to reach this moment. I now hope the police will reopen their inquiries and redouble their efforts to find my wife's killers.'

I have never seen them again since, and the killer or killers were never apprehended. Somebody out there must know something, and I wonder if anybody will ever come forward with new evidence; it's such a tragic story that still saddens me when I think about it.

Chapter Four

I was passing by Tony's room one morning, just before Easter, and he beckoned me in. On the table it looked like he had bundles of money rolled up in elastic bands, and he threw one at me and said, 'Happy Easter Tommy.' Fuck, I was well pleased. 'Nice one, this will come well in handy.' He then waved me away and carried on counting money, lost in his own thoughts.

I went up to my room and took the elastic band off, and counted £300; a nice start for the Easter holidays, he didn't have to do that. I must have caught him in a good mood. I stuck the money in my drawer, took a score out, and headed down the stairs out on to Portobello. I had a drink with the pre-Easter crowd in the Castle.

The following day I thought to give him something. I had read the cult classic book *Snowblind* by Robert Sabbag, set in the cocaine trade in the seventies, many times; I usually had an old copy. When it was first published in the mid-seventies, *Snowblind* established itself as an essential piece of true crime writing. The story of the legendary Zachary Swan, a mover in the cocaine trade in the sixties who set the standard for all who followed, Sabbag's riveting account is a compulsive insight into an underworld populated by crazy characters and driven by paranoia. The result is an illuminating and wild book that influenced a generation of writers and smugglers.

Howard Marks had written the international bestseller *Mr. Nice*, which describes his years as one of the world's most-wanted drug barons. It has sold over one million copies worldwide. I had both *Snowblind*, and *Mr. Nice*. I usually passed them on to people who were interested in adventure and drugs - I gave Tony both copies, it was the least I could do, and I was sure he would enjoy them.

Every day brought something new; there were shoplifters operating all over Notting Hill, feeding their drug habits, and you could buy anything from them. Prostitutes who walked openly around Westbourne Park, Queensway, looking for punters who could help to pay for their crack and smack habits; everybody's got to make a living, everybody was up to something. The well-heeled customers that go in The Cow, run by Tom Conran, oblivious to it all. Sitting outside drinking their gin and tonics eyeing up the customers, to see who could be useful to further their careers in film, fashion, music. A great pub, The Cow; Tom Conran trained as a chef in Paris, in 1995, and launched The Cow gastropub. It's located at 89 Westbourne Park Road, W2.

'Reality is just a crutch for people who just can't cope with drugs'

- Robin Williams

Cocaine is plentiful; the trust fund kids would spend thousands before daddy sent them off to rehab clinics in America or South Africa, and they would come back six months later all clean and serene. Within days, they would be back partying; after all, what else could they do with the £10,000 a month their parents doled out to keep them in pocket money? Most had gone to private schools and felt they were above everybody, ringing their dealers who would turn up in an instant because they knew there was money to be made. Life in Notting Hill is far from boring; there was always money to be made off somebody. They went off to sunnier climes in the wintertime; they travelled extensively and could talk on any subject, well-heeled and privately educated, life was one big party for them.

At the other extreme, beggars galore walk the streets; 'Have you got a pound for a cup of tea?' - you knew full well it was going to be spent on a bag of smack, it's a numbers game, as they walk off in a daze, whether you gave them money or not, looking for the next gullible passerby. There are all kinds of people walking the streets of Notting Hill, Queensway, Westbourne Park.

It is easy to buy cheap tobacco if you know where to go. So many charity shops. Hordes of shoplifters would go into Harrods, in Knightsbridge, stealing anything they could sell on. Pickpockets looking to relieve you of your valuables, sneak thieves entering hotel rooms looking for computers or money you had left around.

That's what makes me laugh when I think about the film *Notting Hill*. I suppose that does go on if you were part of the middle class and upper classes. The cocaine dealers drive around in their nice cars with a gang of young pretty coke whores, who would give a quick blow job, for one more line, to keep the buzz going. I saw and heard all the stories that were going on in the area, the ones in the know knew where to look. You also had the ponces who never did anything, freeloading their way through life with only one aim, to get pissed or high on other people's money. The pubs were full of failed actors or musicians, who got by on what they could blag out of you.

The Road To A Friend's Door Is Never Long

Tony was banging on my door. 'Tommy!' he was shouting. I rolled out of my bed and answered the door.

'What's up Tony?'

'Do you know where that scouse fucker the Assassin has gone?' He looked like he was ready to kill somebody. 'I ordered ten kilos a week ago, to drop off, and I've not heard fuck all since. I've been going around his studios every day and the place is locked up and no fucker there, I've got customers waiting ready with cash, I promised them I would have it for them this week.'

I hadn't seen him for a few months. I never took much notice at the time; people are always saying they are going to leave Portobello Prison, as we called the area, some left, other people came here and never left Portobello Road for years, if ever.

Tony was fuming. I went back to my bed and lay down thinking thank fuck I'm not involved. Months went by with still no sign of the Assassin. Tony had calmed down by then. Life returned to normal; he carried on with his business and I carried on with mine.

On the grapevine, I had heard that the Assassin had bought a one-way ticket to Thailand and found work at a dojo on one of the islands and couldn't return. It was a shame; I had liked the Assassin. Somebody else would replace him for sure; there was always someone who would spot a business opportunity in the borough.

'Dreams don't work unless you do'
- The Wizard of Hampstead, Rainbow George Weiss

Hampstead is an area in north London, England. Lying 4 miles northwest of Charing Cross, it extends from the A5 road (Roman Watling Street) to Hampstead Heath, a large, hilly expanse of parkland, and is known for its intellectual, liberal, artistic, musical, and literary associations. It has some of the most expensive housing in the London area. Hampstead has more millionaires within its boundaries than any other area of the United Kingdom.

Rainbow George was Peter Cook's neighbour and shared the drunken afternoons of his final years. He preserved their conversations on hundreds of hours of tape - the real-life Derek and Clive. George was an interesting character; I had met him back in 1999, he was 60 then. He had set up the Rainbow Party in 1985, which was all about getting rid of politicians - all good by me - for the people to start governing themselves; it may have been a pipe dream although he pursued it with a vengeance. George was Jewish, and his family had fled from Austria during World War Two.

His father had been a diamond dealer in Hatton Garden, and wanted him to follow in his footsteps. He did until he hit 35, when after taking acid his life changed completely. That's when he set up the Rainbow Party.

I did loads of gigs with George. He brought over Ben Reel from Castleblayney in Ireland, where my mother had been born. Ben is a great singer. At the time, George was penniless; he had claimed squatters' rights on his place in Hampstead. His landlord had gone missing. George had not paid any rent in over 12 years.

George won the case, and he was elated. He promised me a small cut if I could find a buyer for his home, so I set out to find a buyer for his gaff in Hampstead.

I would talk to anybody or anyone. A few weeks later, I met an Indian guy, originally from Manchester, who had set up a pop-up shop in Queensway. I told him all about George and his property in Hampstead, and it turned out he was a property developer and had the cash. After months of haggling with George he bought it off him for £700,000.

For the past 20 years, George Weiss had lived on the breadline. His home was in one of London's most salubrious streets but behind the front door was a damp and dilapidated squat.

George rang me and said, 'Tommy, I have just deposited £9000 in your bank.' Wow! Nice one George. I was ecstatic! I gave my sister half and paid off debts I owed.

I thought back to two years earlier, when George had stood in the Brent by-elections, at Brent Town Hall, in September 2003. I was tripping on magic mushrooms in Camden which I had bought from a stall in the market. George rang me to tell me to come down and see the results readout.

I turned up with my *Trainspotting* top on, my hair down my back, sunglasses on, just out of jail for drug smuggling. I followed George onto the stage where the results would be told, standing on the podium with all the press. George told me he had £100 on Sarah Tether to win at 6/1. George loves gambling.

George and I were standing behind Sarah. I was hallucinating on the mushrooms. Sarah Tether won the election. I raised my arm in a victory salute, I was made up George had won £600. Winning the election made political history: it was the first time Labour had won in 15 years and the press went wild. Hundreds of photographers were taking photos.

George and I, who had been standing behind Sarah Tether, were caught in the public eye by the TV stations and newspapers. It was being shown on all the news channels all day. My daughter was in the hospital and having her first son when she saw me on TV. The next day my photo turned up on the front page on the *London Evening Standard*, giving the victory salute, standing behind Sarah Tether. On 19th September 2003, my grandson

Barclay was born; what a coincidence. George and I had some adventures, that's the way I always looked at things.

'Music gives a soul to the universe, wings to the mind, flight to the imagination and life to everything'
- Plato

I was always doing fundraising gigs. I believed it was good for my karma. I enjoy helping people, it gives you a certain feel-good factor; if I can, I will help anybody. I was not a saint, but I was turning my life around. I started getting involved with Tavistock Festival, auditioning bands and singers, holding them at the Mau Mau Bar. I discovered some amazing singers.

Tavistock Festival (London) was a community association of residents and traders working towards supporting local talent by hosting an annual event. Established in 2004, it is a family event to quell the hangover of The Notting Hill Carnival as one final free festival with fun, food and frills for the family.

It brought people from all over and was a huge success.

'Liberty is a different kind of pain from prison'
- T.S. Elliot

I had spent years with conmen, drug dealers, football hooligans. I much prefer creative people these days. I tried my hand at all kinds of things. I was in a play, and I did some extra work for television, appearing in *Casualty* and *Judge John Deed*. I played a prison officer in one scene and it made my father laugh! I wasn't making much money, but I was much happier. I still smoke weed, and I find it helps with my creativity. I had a series of one-night stands; to be honest, I'm much happier in a relationship with somebody I love, but I don't dwell on it. I'm not interested in people just because of money; if they have it, fine, if not, that's fine too.

Walking home one night, steaming drunk around 2am in the morning coming from a gig at the Paradise bar over the Harrow Road way, I accidentally bumped into somebody who shouted 'Watch where you're going!' I muttered sorry; next thing I knew the guy smacked me in the gob I went down. I was so bladdered it took me a while to get back on my feet. It sobered me up though. My mobile had fallen out of my pocket and was in the road, and the guy picked it up and said 'Come and get it you northern bastard' and ran off laughing. I was too hammered to give chase and just thought, fuck it, and staggered on home to my gaff.

I woke up the next day and the side of my face was throbbing like fuck - I blamed myself for being so stupid. I could have kicked myself for losing my phone. I was in a panic; all my contacts were in there. I went to the bathroom and splashed some cold water on my face. I looked a freaking mess and I went back to bed. I just wasn't in the mood to face the day. Just my luck, I thought. Oh well, it could have been worse, people can get stabbed in this city over the most trivial bullshit. I fell back to sleep.

Later that evening I ventured out to the local boozer, the Castle, and had a quick beer. To brighten up my mood, one of the local Moroccans who used to mug people on the street - his nickname was Mush - walked in, and I thought here we go, he's going to try and strong-arm me for a few quid. He was the sort of guy who when he came in the pub, you drank your beer up and fucked off; it just wasn't worth the hassle being around him. He was well known in the area for causing trouble. He came over to me and said 'Hey scouse, do you want to buy a phone?' He called me scouse even though I'm not. Fuck me dead, he pulled out a phone and I could tell it was mine, it was one of those little Nokias only worth a tenner. He laughed when I told him it was mine; he threw it on my table and said 'Yes I know,' and walked out.

I just thought fuck you and laughed to myself. I had my phone back, and the last thing I wanted was to be in a brawl with this lunatic. Deep down I had to admire his cheek; he didn't have to give it me back, but he did. So in a strange kind of way we were friends. I had run-ins with him over the years, and he was always in jail. You wouldn't see him for months or years; he loved crack cocaine would do anything to get his hands on money to score, probably a decent guy if he ever sorted his head out. I went back home, glad I had my phone back - God works in mysterious ways.

Steve Dior

I first met Steve Dior when he had just come back to London from living in Los Angeles. He lived in the Clearlake Hotel of High Street Kensington. Steve had been the front man for the London Cowboys. He came back from America with a young girl called Kelly Pizzo who could sing. They had a great song, 'Dope Fiend', so I decided to manage them. Steve had history. He had lived in New York and played with many great musicians including Sid Vicious, Glen Matlock, Mick Jones, and members of the New York Dolls. Steve had sprung out of the punk scene of '76. He was and still is a great songwriter. When I met him in 2007 Steve was polite, intelligent, and a great singer, and we hit it off. We became friends.

Kelly, a good-looking girl of 22, could really sing. She was a bit shy performing live, but Steve would coax her to come out and play. They were in love; Steve had good taste in women. I learned a lot from Steve over the years. He was a bit of a hermit, but when he came out to play a gig, he was always entertaining and good fun to be around. After six months Kelly went back to Los Angeles. We were both sad to see her go. She had played a few gigs and Steve tried to put a band around her, but in the end, she went back to LA.

Steve had a nephew, Daniel, who had a girlfriend, Rosie, and her younger brother Sid was a drummer. Steve persuaded Sid to play in his band The Delinquents. Sid brought in his schoolmates. Edd Whyte was on guitar, quiet, shy, and noticeably young; people say he looks like Johnny Thunders from the New York Dolls, and he does. Sam Rutland was on bass; he was a classically trained pianist and could play bass too. He was a very striking young man and a bright boy. Steve was 49. He had a band of kids behind him and he taught them a lot. There was a musical legacy stretching back to the Sex Pistols that was being passed on to the new generation. The Delinquents was up and running.

They played quite a few gigs around London in Camden and East London, and then I secured them a six months residency at the infamous Cock Tavern in Kilburn. Kilburn is an area of North London; it has London's highest Irish population, as well as a sizeable Afro-Caribbean population. The first night we played there they found a headless body in a skip up the road. It was rough and ready, just like the band, but over the course of six months, they honed their chops. We had a good laugh; the pub was full of drunks and drug dealers and that was just the bar staff! We had some funny nights down there.

The actor Rik Mayall came one night. Sid the drummer was his son, but Sid didn't really like people knowing. I was standing outside chatting with Rik one night when some old drunk punched Rik in the face for no reason. I'll give Rik his due, he said nothing and just took it in his stride and carried on laughing. The Mayalls are good people.

Edd, Sam, and Sid were having fun; playing every week was good for them. Steve had a habit of falling in and out of smack; he never did it around the kids though. I'd spent a few months around Steve in his room at the Clearlake, and I'd still had the urge every now and then. Steve probably thought I was a novice, but I would smoke with him sometimes. Steve was a good friend and could tell great stories of the music business. It was good to be around him.

The landlady was sound. It wasn't long before Tony was supplying the pub with coke, Es and acid and we had some insane nights in there, all night lock-ins. Sid, Edd, and Sam on bass were only around 17 in those days. They put on some great shows; Steve Dior was out of his head most of the time, but he always performed a great show. It was like being back in the pub rock days of the 70s, wild and pure madness, and the decor of the pub felt like you were in a time warp. Transported back to the 70s.

Coming out of there one night we were at the traffic lights, and somebody was being held up at gunpoint near a cash point, probably some desperado looking for crack money. The lights changed to green and we drove off laughing. Kilburn reminds me of the run-down streets of New York. Hookers roved around, high on smack, looking for some soft twat to put them up against a wall;

pull their knickers up afterward and go searching for the nearest dealers.

It started to get really good down there; we were having fun. More importantly, the band was getting tight. After the six months were up, on the final night, some passer-by threw a brick through the huge front window and it came crashing down on the stage; talk about going out with a bang.

Through Steve I met his very old friend the punk photographer Peter Gravelle. We got on like a house on fire. He had been friends with Sid Vicious, who had died in 1979, and Peter and Steve had great stories about those days back in New York. I was engrossed listening to them. Peter was a cool character who lived in West Kensington, a nice area of London.

I was still booking acts from around London, for the Mau Mau Bar, and the Portobello Gold, owned by Mike Bell. I was getting to know everyone on the scene around London, especially West London.

I had been going to the Gold since the 80s when I lived in Earls Court, and used to visit Veronica, who lived in Ladbroke Grove. It was a great little pub in the heart of Notting Hill. This was where Daniel Craig worked behind the bar years before, where Bill Clinton popped in for a pint when he was President of the USA. Lemmy, from Motorhead, used to drink in there, and play the slot machines. Mike Bell the owner opened the Gold in 1985; it used to be called Princess Alexander before that, where a lot of Hell's Angels hung out.

I got talking to Mike one day, saying I'd like to do music there, and Mike agreed. I started the Sunday nights putting bands on. The night was an instant success. We had some blazing nights there. Hundreds of bands played, including the Alabama 3, who came along and played for my birthday one night.

I started to get to know all the bar staff, who were mainly young and up for a laugh: Steve and Hannah from Sweden, Whiplash, now the lead singer from Pink Cigar, Rob with his swirly moustache.

Mike lived out in Oxford, and usually only came in one or two nights. He left the manager in charge the rest of the time, and there were some deranged times when he wasn't around.

Boss Goodman was the chef upstairs; he had been the main man at Dingwalls Dancehall. He became the roadie for The Deviants, who evolved into The Pink Fairies, the front man for which was Mick Farren. Pink Fairies are an English rock band initially active in the London (Ladbroke Grove) underground and psychedelic scene of the early 1970s. Boss did the booking for Dingwalls, Blondie, The Pretenders, Etta James, and Muddy Waters being just a few he booked back in the day; he was also a DJ and a great chef, a great man.

I have many happy memories of the Portobello Gold and all the staff that worked there including Helena from Sweden, who I got on with. She was in her early twenties, and was going out with Jem from North Wales. He worked with Stage Miracles and had worked all over the world doing stage and lighting shows. He had money to burn. They were both up for a laugh, my kind of people. They also booked gigs and were well into their music big time. There was Raffy from Poland, Ewa from Poland, Tim from Bristol with his mate George, Duggie from New Zealand, Marco from Italy, and Jennifer from Belgium who is now the manager at Ed Sheeran's new pub Bertie Blossoms further up the road on Portobello, which used to be the Spanish Restaurant Galazia back in the day.

I was still wheeling and dealing with weed. I wasn't making a fortune, but I had a few shilling in the bank so I was on my feet. I had worked hard grafting at gigs, making deliveries all over London after building up a large list of punters. I was kept busy in between doing gigs and grafting, I never had much time to myself.

I was doing a couple of gigs a week. Also doing band stuff. I was busy. I met a girl from Slovenia called Lauritia. She was singing with her boyfriend Eddie. We became friends. I started playing the bongos with them in the band. Lauritia had been played on the radio in her native Slovenia when she was 17. She was doing blues and jazz with Eddie. She came to London when she was 21 to nanny and learned about England and the music scene, then after a few years in London, she met Eddie.

I was out all the time, barely getting any rest at all, but I was happy. The Delinquents were playing out a lot, and The Rotten Hill Gang started to form around this time, and I met Gary

64

McPherson. Gary was Mick Jones' right-hand man and had played in Big Audio Dynamite. I started to get to know Gary, he's a funny guy, highly creative, mad about music and the women flock around him. I always found Mick to be a gentleman and very down to earth. To Clash fans, he is a superstar, and I'd like him, even if he weren't in a band.

I love being around music and musicians. There is a great energy; they are all different but the one thing they have in common is a love, a deep passion, for music. I like having a laugh. Some people you gel with, others you don't. In life, you must take the rough with the smooth. I was used to living on the edge, so I was used to living like this.

I wasn't cut out for the 9 to 5. I was living below the margin and my mind was always planning for gigs and thinking about shows. There were always opportunities in London, it was not like being in the middle of nowhere. I was a born hustler, but money isn't my god anymore, just a tool to be used for pleasurable things.

Also at this time I met Dave, and George Vjestica, who went on to play with Nick Cave and the Bad Seeds. Dave and George were a duo for a while. Dave went to America and lived in New York and had a couple of kids. I was meeting loads of creative people.

I remember Ossie Clarke the designer, who had gone to my school in Warrington, Beamont; he had lived around Holland Park before he was murdered by his gay lover. I met him once when he came back for a school reunion, and he inspired me too when I think about it now. He made me realise there was more to life than Warrington, and that you could be different.

'Many friends will walk in and out of your life, but only true friends will leave footprints on your heart'
- Eleanor Roosevelt

I had other friends around Ladbroke Grove who were not involved in music. My long-time friend Rob Taylor, I had known from school days, and we'd come to London together in the 80s. A fanatical Man City fan, he was known as Man City Rob. He had been married to Theresa for years they had two kids, Ruby and Chloe. Rob was a great character who loved his family. Sadly, they separated, but we all still get along. Rob was a painter and decorator, and he loved football, northern soul, and a good punch up if you upset him.

Rob knew everyone around the Grove and introduced me to scouse Kenny. Kenny was a top man, and we had some great laughs over the years. They were northerners who worked on building sites, no airs and graces. I didn't see that much of Rob after he had moved to Kensal Rise. I was always doing music, but when we did meet up it was always fun.

I loved West London, it's a very friendly community, and even though the rich, the poor, the blacks and the whites live side by side, they get on relatively happily. The Royal Borough of Kensington, with its parks and museums, is rich in history and culture. They're gentrifying the area now and driving out the characters, which is such a shame.

Tony came back one night and asked me to come in his room. He closed the door and said 'Listen, Tommy, I will be pulling out of London soon and you will have to look for another place to live.' I had been living at his gaff 4 years by then. He gave me 4 weeks to find another place to crash.

Tony hinted he was going to be leaving London and going overseas somewhere. I asked him where and he said it was best I didn't know. Ok, I thought, he was probably right.

Luckily, I found a place to sublet over in Queens Park, and moved in when the time came. I was sad to be leaving, but I had no choice in the matter.

When I moved out, Tony pulled a fast move a few days later and vanished, never to be seen again; that is life living in London: friendships can be forged and lost in an instant. Wherever he is, I'm sure he will be having the time of his life.

If nothing else I was keeping myself busy, looking for venues, sourcing bands, and keeping my eye on any opportunities that might arise. Walking along the borough you could often catch the sweet smell of skunk wafting through the air; somebody close by was having a smoke. Mainly the young kids were now smoking it, replacing the hash of their fathers' generation; it was so strong that was all they wanted and there was always somebody who had kilos of the stuff ready to shift to the ever-growing market.

The Vietnamese had cornered the market renting houses and starting to grow in rented houses; serious money was being made. There are so many street gangs all over London, the Albanians running the coke, the Italian Mafia, the Russians, the Somalians, the Triads from China, the Yakuza from Japan, the Bengalis: they are all fighting over the drug trade on the streets of the capital. London is very safe if you know where to go, but it can also be very dangerous if you become involved in the drug trade on a large scale. You could easily end up in the hospital or the mortuary for your efforts.

Music and drugs went hand in hand. Nearly all the musicians I knew would smoke and some of them were on harder drugs. It helped with their creativity; the days of rock and roll excesses are far from over, although the big money made by the bands of the 70s is well gone, and the record companies won't tolerate it these days, they want young bands to do all the work and toe the line, be clean-cut and professional. The chosen few like the Stones and Elton John can still fill stadiums, gigantic money-making machines; the young teenage bands coming through can only dream of making it that big.

Rock and Roll is becoming marginalised to the little clubs these days. A bit like jazz, it's probably had its heyday, and not many interesting characters are left in the mainstream. At least Liam and Noel, with their constant rows through the media, make for a bit of light entertainment.

I would go often to see Dandi, and his new Swedish girlfriend Kiki, who became friends. Kiki was of Indian descent; their place was highly creative, and they kept it spotless. They always made me welcome and it was a little oasis from the bustle of city life.

Dandi had the look of Ronnie Wood, and was constantly playing the bass, although he had given up being in a band. After the last fiasco with NRG Fly, he vowed never to join a band again. Which was a shame; they had been a great little outfit, and David Caplin, the guitar player, had now done his rehab to get over his smack and crack problem and really started to get his head together. He set up a building company and started to make good money, which was good to see, as he had been in a right mess before I got lifted in Jamaica. Andy, the lead singer, had opened a small studio off the All Saint's Road and was now using his skills to record other bands.

Stupidly I got involved with a deal with an Irish guy called Damian, who told me he could get some really nice Thai weed at a good price, £1400 on the kilo; I trusted him. It was all the money I could scrape together. I had met him through Tony, my mate. Damian had the blarney and could talk people into anything; he said he had to get the money upfront, and he would collect it over in North London. I should have gone with him to collect it, but I trusted him, and gave him the readies; big mistake on my part, it was the last I ever saw of my money, or him. I couldn't believe my luck; how had I been so stupid? I was kicking myself for weeks, I was back on my arse and things were not looking good. I thought my luck couldn't get any worse.

'If things go wrong, don't go with them'
- Roger Babson

Chapter Five

I was wrong: more bad luck came my way. I was living in a flat in Queens Park, but the guy I was subletting from wanted it back, so once again I had to leave. I had nowhere to go and was pretty destitute by this time. I had to go cap in hand to the HPU, the Homeless Persons Unit of the Council, and throw myself on their mercy.

I spent all day at the offices in High Street Kensington before they decided I would be offered temporary accommodation in a hotel in Bayswater. I was well and truly grateful they had decided to give me a roof over my head for up to six weeks. While they decided what to do with me, being a single man, they didn't hold out much hope for me getting a place out of it at the end of the six weeks.

I went straight from the council offices, along High Street Kensington, and cut through Hyde Park, to make my way to arrive in Bayswater, at the hotel on Queens Drive, clutching my white form to let them know who I was. When I got there, it was a rundown hotel, with a green and white awning outside. I was to sign in and out each day in the register, so the council could keep tabs on me. The Indian guy who was running the place explained it to me. In the foyer were a lot of Somalians who were staying in the hotel, sitting around chewing on Khat, the leafy green plant that comes from Africa, and has a similar effect to taking speed. They all started chatting in Somali and pointing at me and laughing, surprised to see a white guy down on his luck. I couldn't understand what they were saying. I was sure they were taking the piss. I sometimes look back on these experiences and wish I had taken photos: 'Look at me now Ma, on top of the world.'

The Indian guy gave me the keys for my room. I was up on the second floor. I could hear a couple in the next room banging

69

and shouting at each other; it sounded Arabic. I turned the key in the door and my heart sank: it stunk of piss and had no windows. It looked like they had put me in the broom cupboard. There was a table and a chair. On the table somebody had left a small copy of the Koran; I picked it up and flipped through it, but much like the Bible it was all nonsense to me. I put it down, decided I was going to get my head down and just flopped out on the single bed and lay there thinking, what the fuck have I got myself into. I was now living like the proverbial starving artist myself.

I fell asleep that night, but I awoke around 7am, starving. I brushed my teeth and had a wash and tried to make myself presentable; 'Tommy and his tin pot promotions' was back in town, and I was laughing to myself whilst looking at my reflection in the cracked mirror. I was on the slippery slope downwards.

I wandered down the stairs to find the small restaurant that served up breakfast. I walked into the kitchen, and the smell of boiled eggs hit me. On the table was coffee and milk. I picked up a couple of eggs, toast, and jam, and went and found a table to sit down. The room was packed with about 30 people babbling in all kinds of languages. I was the only white face amongst the clientele.

I sat down next to one of the Somalian guys at the only space I could find, and he started to chat with me while I was peeling the shell off my egg. My stomach was turning at the smell of the eggs, it smelt like somebody had stood on a stink bomb. I was on the point of retching, when I pulled myself together, and he asked me if I was Scottish, perhaps because of my ginger hair and northern accent. I just grunted and said I was, I mean what the fuck else was I going to say? He told me his name was Yusuf; he looked around thirtyish, and two of his front teeth were missing. He told me had been in the Hotel for 18 months, and he was hoping to get a place off the council in the next few months. Then he added slyly that if I wanted any weed, to come and see him; he was on the third floor. Ok, I said, with no intention of buying anything from anybody in the hotel: the last thing I wanted was to be getting involved with my neighbours. I decided I would quit coming down for breakfast; the fewer people knew about me the better.

After breakfast I headed out into the street and went for a walk to clear my head and see what was going on. Bayswater and

Queensway are notorious for hookers, and I spotted a couple of Thai ladyboys walking arm in arm, mincing along and chatting Thai with each other, probably off to the many shops to buy new dresses to entice customers that night.

I headed over to Hyde Park. It is one of London's eight Royal Parks and covers an area of 350 acres, a great place for walking; it was still quite early, but even so, loads of tourists were milling about clutching their handbags and backpacks. They had better be careful, I thought, South American pickpockets were renowned to operate all over, and they were experts who had relieved many unsuspecting tourists of their valuables. I was just one of many faces walking the streets. I blended in and nobody really knew me in the area. I enjoyed the anonymity for a change; Portobello Road could be quite claustrophobic at times.

I arrived at Hyde Park and made my way to the Serpentine, where I sat down on one of the many green benches. Watching the tourists feeding the ducks I felt much better. My mind had got rid of the smell of the boiled eggs, at last. I've always had a weak stomach. I sat there for hours thinking, and eventually I walked back towards the hotel. Calling in at Tesco's, I bought cleaning supplies, and decided to give the room a thorough cleaning. I passed Yusuf who was chatting with his mates outside the hotel and went up to the room. I poured bleach all over the floors and mopped up, and when I felt satisfied the smell of piss had gone, I put everything away.

Over the next few weeks I fell in with the rhythm of the hotel. I spent my days walking around Hyde Park, going to gigs in the evenings, and I did lots of reading, picking up cheap books in the charity shops. I read Jean Genet's *The Thief's Journal*, about his life on the streets of France, as a homosexual and petty thief, travelling around Europe. It came out in 1949 and was voted the best book of the year in France. I love true stories; even though it was semi-biographical and part fiction, the man had a way with words.

I had been at the hotel for around 4 weeks when a letter came from the council to tell me I was going to be evicted in 14 days' time. They had decided I could find my own accommodation. It was a shock to the system: I knew it was coming, but I had pushed it to the back of my mind. Now I must take some action.

I went to the Citizens Advice Bureau the next day, and they advised me I should get myself a housing lawyer who specialised in these cases. I made an appointment to go and see a lawyer on Golborne Road. I saw a lady lawyer who advised me I should stay put; they would fight the case on my part and put an appeal in. I readily agreed. To rent a 1 bedroom flat around Notting Hill cost upwards of £350 a week minimum, and you had to put down a month's deposit and a month upfront. I just never had that kind of money. It was a long drawn out process and one I was determined to dig my heels in and fight.

Over the course of the next two years, I had six eviction notices. Each time my barrister fought the case and got me a stay of execution; it was a good job I had the will to fight. It was a very unsettling time in my life. In between I was putting gigs on and trying to keep my head above water.

At the very last minute one time, the day before I was due to be evicted, the barrister got me out of another eviction. They moved me around to different rooms; it became really annoying. I had no choice though but to do as I was told. I wasn't allowed to have visitors in my room, and it was beginning to feel like an open prison; many times I thought it might not be worth all this hassle.

There were times I would have to resort to food banks to keep me going. I was at rock bottom. I never told my family or friends what I was going through, I just soldiered on, hoping my luck would change. London can be a difficult place to survive and many people end up on the streets. You have the genuine people who are down on their luck. You also have the aggressive ones who really were pulling scams, pretending to be homeless when in reality they had flats and even houses to go to. Some of them drove cars, changed their clothes and went out begging on the lucrative streets of the borough. Some were dropped off in vans by unscrupulous gang bosses who forced people to beg; they had no other way to survive, they couldn't speak English and were forced out onto the streets.

There were lots of police patrolling the moneyed streets of Westminster, Kensington and Chelsea, keeping the rich safe in their palatial homes and moving the beggars on. I would shoplift sometimes to get bread and milk to take back to my room. There were no cooking facilities, just a small microwave, and a kettle. There was a cigarette paper separating me from a park bench at times.

Oftentimes I would get half a dozen cans of special brew, go back to my room and get obliterated, waking up the next day feeling like death warmed up, forcing myself out of bed and heading to Hyde Park, looking at the families playing happily, feeling a sense of remorse at how I had ended up in this situation in the first place. I had a handful of friends; they had their own problems. I had outstayed my welcome many times sleeping on friends' sofas.

'The devil finds work for idle hands'
- Biblical quote

After not touching smack for years, I ran into a friend whose street name was Digger, who used to score it all the time. It was like the devil to me, I knew the dangers. I said to him let's go back to yours; lucky for me that I was with my mate Dandi, who came along. He never touches the stuff. It had nearly ended my life a couple of times in my past. Why I wanted it this day I will never know. We went back to Digger's on one of the back roads behind Bayswater.

He took the gear out of a tiny balloon, and I watched with interest while he cooked it up. Injecting heroin is extremely dangerous. It's easier to overdose from injecting than from other ways of taking the drug. I was absorbed while he got the syringe out, which he used to suck up some water and squirt it into the spoon. He then heated the spoon from the bottom with a lighter to make it dissolve better.

He took a piece of cotton and rolled it into a ball a little bigger than a very tiny wad. The cotton was dropped into the heroin and it puffed up. The tip of the syringe was pushed into the centre of the cotton and the plunger was gently pulled back until all the heroin was sucked in.

73

He placed the needle almost flat on his skin, so it didn't wiggle around too much. He stuck the needle in. Usually, it will burn while it's being injected if it's not going in the vein. This is one way to tell if it's not going in the vein. When the needle is inserted, the plunger is pulled slowly a tiny bit to see if blood comes in. This shows that it's in the vein. Sometimes when the plunger is pulled, only a slow trickle of blood comes in and the rest is air.

He inserted it into himself first, and a look of euphoria came over his face after a couple of minutes. I asked him to hit me up. He said 'Are you sure Tommy?' I said yes. I was eager to get high and forget my troubles.

I moved closer, rolled my shirt up and tied a piece of string around my arm, and pulled it tight, so my veins in the crook of my arm would rise ready for the needle to be inserted. He repeated the procedure on me and I remember thinking God that feels so good, it hits you instantly, unlike chasing the dragon where you smoke the powder off tin foil. Then it all went blank.

Dandi told me later my breathing was terribly slow. I had fallen into a coma. I could have died but for the quick thinking of Dandi, who had never taken it in his life. He rang the ambulance. He said later my face and lips were turning blue, and he was slapping my face until I opened my mouth. He placed a spoon under my tongue to stop me from choking.

If I had been taking heroin regularly, I may have built up some tolerance. But it had been quite a few years since I last touched it. If you just stop taking heroin for just a few days, your tolerance can rapidly drop, and you risk an overdose.

Injecting heroin can fuck your veins and arteries, and has been known to lead to gangrene, which I have known people to die from. Dandi said he was panicking in case I died. Digger was panicking in case I died, and he was charged with manslaughter, but it wasn't his fault, it was mine. I knew what I was doing. I couldn't resist the temptation at the time.

Dandi said the paramedics arrived really quickly and pumped me with drugs to reverse the heroin in my bloodstream. They stretchered me out of the flat and I was taken to St Mary's hospital where they brought me back to life. I knew nothing of this.

I had been so unconscious throughout the ordeal that when I came round it took me a few minutes to come to my senses and realise what had happened. I apologised to the nurses and they made me promise I would never touch it again. I gave them a huge thanks. I had been playing Russian Roulette with my life so many times over the years, I realised this had got to be the final wakeup call. I made my mind up there and then that I would never use it ever again. Many people die each year in London from smack, even first-time users; it can be deadly, injecting, especially if you don't know what you are doing, just say no is the only advice I can give. The problem is it can be so nice even from the very first time you try it, you can puke up and feel like shit at the same time but still want to go on and try more, especially if you are insecure; it can wrap its arms around you and suck you in within minutes. It has given people lifetime habits and taken them to hell and back. It can put people in mortuaries, turned them into thieves and prostitutes, all from that very first hit.

I left the hospital the next day feeling like the luckiest man alive; that truly had been a wake-up call that I had needed. I headed back home and have never touched it since. I was never a hardcore user but I had dabbled with it for many years back in the 90s, mainly smoking it off tin foil; but I knew my time was finally over and done with. It was never something I was proud of, it is not a social drug and many users keep it a secret from their friends and stay home feeding their habits in private. It can give you delusions of grandeur when you are on it, you feel anything is possible but deep down you are just deceiving yourself.

'Miss Heroin'
'Take me in your arms, so now, little man, you've grown tired of grass, LSD, cocaine, and hash, and someone, pretending to be a true friend, I'll introduce you to Miss Heroin. Well honey, before you start fooling with me, just let me inform you of how it will be. For I will seduce you and make you my slave, I've sent men much stronger than you to their graves. You think you could never become a disgrace and end up addicted to poppy seed waste.

So you'll start inhaling me one afternoon, you'll take me into your arms very soon. And once I've entered deep down in your veins, the craving will nearly drive you insane. You'll swindle your mother and just for a buck. You'll turn into something vile and corrupt

You'll mug and you'll steal for my narcotic charm and feel contentment when I'm in your arms. The day when you realise the monster you've grown, you'll solemnly swear to leave me alone, you think you've got that mystical knack, then sweetie, just try getting me off your back. The vomit, the cramps, your gut tied in knots. The jangling nerves screaming for one more shot.

The hot chills and cold sweats, withdrawal pains, can only be saved by my little white grains, there's no other way, and there's no need to look, for deep down inside you know you are hooked. You'll desperately run to the pushers and then, you'll welcome me back to your arms once again. And you will return just as I foretold! I know that you'll give me your body and soul. You'll give up your morals, your conscience, your heart. And you will be mine until "Death Do Us Part" '

- Author Unknown

I truly could relate to the old blues and the country singers who I had grown up listening to on my dad's record collection. I was living it.

I started to get to know all the down and outs around the borough. There was one old man from the Czech Republic who used to scour the streets looking for fag ends he would place in his trouser pockets, to smoke later on; his name was Jan, he must have been about 70. He always had a smile on his face. He was a huge man with bright blue eyes, his clothes were tattered, and he wore an old donkey jacket. We would stop and chat. Once or twice he would offer me a roll-up. He had come to London years before, when he had been married. It all fell apart when he lost his job and lost his wife, he hit the booze and ended up on the streets. There are many such cases of real people who are homeless in this city. I suppose it was my pride that stopped me going back to the north of England and looking like a failure. I would get through this period of my life somehow and come through a better man because of it, I told myself.

Back at the hotel there were arguments, doors banging, day and night sometimes. I felt like I was in a madhouse. Tenants came and went; some of them looked like dodgy fuckers; half of them were dealing one thing or the other.

The Somalians were on Khat all the time. I felt safer outside on the streets more often than being in my room. I was still wheeling and dealing when I met tourists who were looking to score some weed. One time I was so skint, some Americans who were passing through asked me to score some good shit, and I went around the corner, got some tree bark and broke it up, sealed it in clingfilm, went back and told them this was the best shit in the area; they handed me £20 and I told them to enjoy it. I felt guilty. I could imagine them back in their room trying to light the spliff up. I learned that trick from an old Jamaican friend of mine, Killer; aw fuck it, I had to survive.

In the night times I would wander around just to get out of the room. Prostitutes would accost me looking for business, and I would shake my head and say 'No money.' The smiles they gave me would drop instantly as they looked straight through me for further punters. Having no cash can strip you of your confidence, not me though. At least you knew who your real friends were in these times and I concluded I was lucky I had any.

After the accidental overdose, it took me a few days to get my head together. I was getting tired of living in the hotel and was hoping to get out of there. Money was so tight my clothes were threadbare; I was trawling the charity shops looking for bargains. How the mighty had fallen with a crashing bang. Luckily my head was strong, I had no need for the finer things in life. Had never been my style anyway, I came from the first-up best-dressed era back when I was a kid. I hadn't been brought up with a silver spoon in my mouth, more like dragged up, although it stood me in good stead over the years, some of the crazy situations I had found myself in.

The Somalian guy Yusuf was getting on my tits, hovering around, sticking his nose in my business. I often felt he was watching me to see if I had anything in my room worth stealing, which made me laugh. He may have got a few pot noodles. I would buy 14 of them to last me a fortnight; I hate them now although they were my main hot meal of the day back then. I started to score weed from the travellers over Bethnal Green way, which is an area in the East End of London centred a mile from Liverpool Street station.

They had good skunk, I had been told, at reasonable prices. They were mainly Irish, rough as fuck. I sometimes felt like I was taking my life in my hands.

Arriving at the camp, half a dozen of them would surround me, checking me out. A mate of mine had put me in contact with them and vouched for me so the main man on the camp trusted me. I had scraped a few quid together and he sorted me out with a few ounces. He was a big fucker with a beard and had the look of a brawler, which all the travellers were anyway, desperate men do desperate things. His name was Sean. He would take me into his caravan and tell the others to fuck off. He had a small safe stuffed with cash and drugs; I couldn't see anybody robbing him anytime soon.

He would weigh the weed out in front of me and take the cash with a smile on his face. I ended up going back there quite a lot over the next few months. I always felt a bit uneasy around them and carrying the skunk back on the tube was a bit risky as it stunk to high heaven. Sometimes you would have the police at the tube stations with dogs. So I would get on the buses; it was a ball ache, but I had to do it. I got on the phone and let a few people know, and it sold like a best seller when I got back in West London.

I would weigh it up in my room on the small scales. I had to wrap it up in cling film and start moving it as quickly as possible. People started coming to the hotel and waiting outside; I was back in business. The Somalians knew I was up to something, fuck them, it was none of their business. I started building up a new clientele around Bayswater; drugs open doors for you, people recommend you and it took you into the homes of the extremely wealthy along with the council estates. I didn't give a toss. I wanted the money.

Within a couple of months, I found a new source to get the weed from. I was getting tired of the schlep up to East London and dealing with the travellers was no joke. I met a girl from Bristol who had set up shop in Notting Hill. She was good looking and shrewd, and she only opened a couple of days a week between certain times. I would turn up and half a dozen of her customers would be lined up waiting to go in and collect their weed.

I was turning over a few quid and keeping active around the borough; things were looking up. I started eating in the Spanish cafe and fucked the pot noodles off. I had a belly full of them to last me a lifetime. I was shifting to a lot of musicians, and anybody else who had the paperwork. I would go anywhere and deliver to Knightsbridge, South Kensington, Fulham, Chelsea, Camden, Hampstead. I acquired a pushbike off one of my punters in exchange for some weed. If you have never been skint, good for you. I have been on my arse loads of times and weed always pulled me out of a hole.

A letter came from the council. They had decided I would be eligible for social housing, but first I must go to a halfway house. I was excited I would be getting out of the hotel and there was a glimmer of hope that I could end up with my own place on a decent rent agreement.

I packed my meagre belongings and made my way to Barlby Road. Two years had flown by since I had first arrived at the hotel. I was glad to be out of there. I caught the bus. It was a couple of miles away. I was back in the borough of Kensington and Chelsea.

When I arrived there, I was met by Andrew, a Kiwi social worker who had an office in the building. He told me the rules of the house and said his office would be manned between 9 and 5 and if I had any problems I could come and chat. Then he showed me my room. I was pleasantly surprised; it had been freshly painted. I had windows with a clean single bed. It looked like you could swing a couple of cats in there. It was spacious and I was well happy.

The building was just behind the mental health hospital, St Charles. I would meet some of the patients when I went to the local shops. West London has the highest concentration of Care in the Community than anywhere else in the UK. I felt at home.

79

Care in the Community is the British policy of deinstitutionalisation: treating and caring for physically and mentally disabled people in their homes rather than in an institution.

'Reflective thinking turns experience into insight'
- John C Maxwell

I'd first met Lauritia and Eddie in 2005. Lauritia was an award-winning jazz singer with over 10 years of performing experience in the UK and around Europe. I met Lauritia again, at a party; she had split up from Eddie, and she was with her friend Debbie. I decided to walk her home to Neasden. We became friends at first, as she needed time to get over Eddie. As time went by, we became lovers. Lauritia had a calming effect on me and didn't smoke or drink much; she was great company. When Eddie found out he never spoke to me again, silly really. I was ducking and diving from the halfway house, going to see her, putting gigs on, and hoping to get a flat out of the halfway house.

I went to meet her parents in Slovenia. They were good people. We were taking things slowly. She loved singing and performing but was not one for going out a lot. This suited me as it allowed me to get on with the music business, with her calming influence behind me. It's good to keep your private life private.

Steve and the Delinquents were playing lots of gigs. They played for the Hell's Angels down in Bristol, a fucked-up night that was! They played under the Westway before they made it into Acklam Village Market. They would play at the Portobello Gold for a Sunday dinner and a few quid. It was great for the band, they were learning their trade, paying their dues, and having fun on top of it all.

Ticker and Trouble

I had a really strange feeling one day in the summer of 2007. I felt really out of sorts, sweating, walking through Bayswater, on my way to see Dandi. I couldn't catch my breath. I saw a chemist was open so I walked in and explained to the chemist how I was feeling. She said it sounds like you are having a heart attack; what the fuck I thought, and sat down on a chair while she called an ambulance, which came along five minutes later. They put me on a stretcher and drove me off to St Mary's Hospital.

With the sirens blaring, we got there, and they immediately wheeled me into the operating theatre, where the doctor looked me over and said we will have to operate on you now. My mind was racing, not sure what to think, was this it? Was my life going to be over? I was confused. The doctor explained I was going to have angioplasty surgery and stents would be inserted. Angioplasty and stent insertion is used to treat narrowing in an artery. Angioplasty uses a small, sausage-shaped balloon to stretch the artery open and improve blood flow. The stent is a small metal cylinder that acts as a scaffold to hold the artery permanently open. Angioplasty is the name of the procedure carried out with the assistance of an angiogram, a special kind of X-ray image or picture that shows the arteries live on a screen.

The operation starts with an angiogram and is carried out through a skin puncture into the blood vessel that feeds the narrowed or diseased vessels. Most often, the skin puncture is in the groin, at the top of the leg. Less commonly, you may need to have the skin puncture in your upper arm, if the blood vessel in the groin cannot be used.

A liquid contrast agent (sometimes referred to as contrast medium or dye) is injected into the artery to show the blood vessels on an X-ray image. Without contrast injection, blood vessels are invisible on X-rays. Angioplasty and stent insertion is carried out using the live images that are displayed on a television screen to guide the procedure.

A local anaesthetic is injected into the skin and soft tissues, and around the artery that will be used to gain access to the blood vessels that require treatment. This artery is usually the one in front of the hip or groin region, called the femoral artery. A needle is passed into the anaesthetised artery and then a soft and flexible guide wire is passed through the needle into the artery. A sheath is then passed over the wire and into the artery. The sheath is a plastic tube with a tap on one end. It usually measures 2–3 mm (1/8 inch) in diameter. Once the sheath is in place, the balloons and stents are all passed through this sheath.

A very thin tube is then passed through the sheath into the narrowed artery and an angiogram picture is taken. Using this picture, the correct sized balloon is chosen. Angioplasty is carried out by passing a thin tube into the artery. The tube is called a balloon angioplasty catheter and has an inflatable balloon on the end of it. The balloon is shaped like a long sausage when it is inflated. The correct balloon size is selected for the artery being treated. The balloon is inflated where the artery is narrow and stretches the artery up to normal size. This procedure can be carried out for arteries almost anywhere in the body. After the balloon has been inflated for up to 3 minutes, it is deflated and removed. Another tube is passed into the artery to inject contrast medium. The contrast medium is injected while X-rays are being taken to provide an angiogram showing images of the new shape of the artery.

Sometimes, the angioplasty is enough to keep the artery open, but on many occasions, a stent is required to hold it open. A stent is a metal tube that is inserted into the artery through the same sheath in the groin region. It acts as a scaffold to prevent the narrow section of the artery collapsing back. A stent stays in the artery permanently.

The sheath is removed from the groin and an arterial closure device is sometimes inserted to close the artery and stop the bleeding. Alternatively, pressure (either with the doctor's or nurse's finger over the puncture site or with a clamp) is applied to the puncture site to stop the artery from bleeding. You must lie flat for between 1 and 4 hours after this.

I lay on the operating table watching all this happening. It took about an hour and finally they trundled me out and put me in a hospital bed on one of the wards. That night the surgeon came to see me and told me I was incredibly lucky to be alive; if I had come an hour later, I would have been dead; fuck, that was close, I thought.

I spent the next 8 days in recovery at the hospital. Rob came to see me. We had a good laugh that I was still alive and kicking. My brother Anthony drove up from Warrington to see me. He said he was going to book me a holiday in Thailand to recover when I got out. Nice one Anthony, I was well pleased.

I had a massive bruise on my leg, but I felt fine and ready for a good holiday. I would be on medication for life, but I was still around to tell the tale.

A few weeks later, I told the social worker my brother was taking me on holiday. He agreed I needed one. True to his word, Anthony booked the holiday, with his mate Chris from Warrington and my mate from school days Paul, who boarded the plane in Dubai where he was working at the time and landed in Bangkok. I was looking forward to 3 weeks of recuperation, but I think they had other things on their minds.

We quickly booked into a couple of hotels, and proceeded to go out that night. They got hammered but I tried to take it easy and kept a close eye on them. The hookers are plentiful in Bangkok, and as soon as they saw us with our white legs, they knew we were fair game, ripe to be relieved of our money.

It's quite comical really, but it felt good to be back in Thailand after an 8 year absence. I still had memories of the Thai jail I had spent time in, years before, and fully intended not to end up there again. We did the usual rounds of Patpong 1 and 2, and nothing much had changed in the preceding years, or so I thought. Later that night we got a few tuk tuks back to the hotel and hit the sack. In the morning we booked a flight to take us to the island of Koh Samui, and took a taxi to the domestic airport later that afternoon. We were all buzzing to be getting out of the city, it was so hot, and looking forward to hitting the beaches of Lamai, which had been my home all those years ago.

Ko Samui (or Koh Samui, also often locally shortened to Samui) Thai is an island off the east coast of Thailand. We landed in the small airport with its breathtaking views; you feel like you are in paradise on arrival. We jumped into one of the island taxis and headed for Lamai beach to my friend's Sunrise Bungalows - I had not seen Phum for over 8 years. She laughed when we arrived and said 'No late parties, Tommy, we have better rooms now and no budget travellers these days either, people come for two weeks and spend lots of money' - ever the businesswoman, she checked us in. We took the A-frame bungalows very close to Lamai Beach. We were all pretty shattered. I threw my bag into the room, got changed and went for a dip in the warm waters of the Gulf of Thailand.

There were a lot more tourists than I remembered from my last visit. I was only here for 3 weeks and intended to mainly chill. I had been coming to Thailand for over 30 years, and knew Koh Samui very well. Phum and her family had been born on the island, back when it was a sleepy little village. Fishermen and coconuts were the mainstay of income in those days until the hippies started arriving in 1975, and then Western and European backpackers and adventurers started coming to the pristine paradise of Koh Samui, quickly establishing it as a hidden secret for beach lovers.

At first, visitors had to sleep out on the beach, in hammocks, or in simple bungalows, but soon, the islanders extended their hospitality (and saw the opportunity) by starting simple guesthouses, restaurants, and other services for the foreigners. Right through the rest of the 1970s and 80s Koh Samui, with its hippy vibe and basic, humble accommodation, which was certainly very different to what you will find on the island today, continued to be popular amongst those travellers who were in search of a real escape and tropical island getaway.

Chris, Paul, and our kid went exploring and I went to sleep on the beach. I woke a few hours later with a voice calling my name. It was Kat, one of the beach sellers; he was about 25 now. 'Tommy, good to see you, long time no see my friend.' I bought a hammock off him, and he told me he was married now with children. We spent half an hour reminiscing about the past. When he used to work for me, bringing tourists to the bar and selling merchandise, I had to pinch myself at times; living in paradise had been fun.

That evening we ate in the restaurant that overlooked the sea. Phum came over afterward and we chatted about how things had changed since I had last been here. I asked her if she had heard anything about Mentona K, and what she told me surprised me.

She said a couple of months after I left the island, he had been arrested for selling cocaine and the police took him and three other Africans to the mainland of Surat Thani. She hadn't heard what had happened since then.

It all made sense now; he had been involved in drugs and was probably languishing in some Thai snake pit somewhere. It wasn't unknown for tourists to get jailed for 50 years in Thailand for drug offences. It's well known that the Nigerians run a drug-smuggling ring all through Asia. They pay for Africans to come from their homelands. Then make them become smugglers, and if they are caught, they are on their own and spend years in prison; a sad tale but human life is very cheap to these gangsters.

The Nigerians were the worst throughout Asia. They had a thing called the Black Money Scam, the blag, sometimes known as the 'wash scam', where con artists attempt to fraudulently obtain money from a victim by convincing him or her that piles of banknote-sized paper in a suitcase are actually currency notes that have been dyed to avoid detection by authorities. The victim is persuaded to pay fees and purchase chemicals to remove the dye, with the promise of a share in the proceeds back in the States or wherever the mark came from. In the bars of Bangkok, they would have spotters out looking for mugs who they could fleece, it was such a crazy little scam. They would wheel them in and tell them they were going to make millions bringing it through customs, in a huge suitcase full of black paper they had painted.

Authentic US$100 bills are coated with a protective layer of glue and then dipped into a solution of iodine. The bill, when dried, looks and feels like black sugar paper. The mass of notes is real sugar paper; when the victim picks a 'note' for cleaning, it is switched with the iodine coated note. The 'magic cleaning solution' is crushed Vitamin C tablets dissolved in water.

Somebody always fell for it; they were smooth and plausible. They tried it on me, but I could tell it was a blag and fucked them off. I met some of them when I was banged up in Thailand, years before, roaming around the jail with a Bible in their hands; they used to make me laugh, ultra-smooth con men, I suppose it was ingrained in their psyche.

The next 3 weeks passed by, and we had fun, but now it was time to leave. We had a 3-day stopover in Dubai on the way back, staying at Paul's villa. My brother Anthony loved it, vowing to return to Dubai, soon.

On the final night, we made our way back to the airport in Dubai. I took my flight back to London, and our kid and his mate took the flight back to Manchester.

'Don't listen to what they say, go see'
- Chinese proverb

My son Tommy was born at 8:10am Saturday 12th April 2008, in St Mary's Hospital, Paddington. My sister Lynn was there. I was the proudest man on earth. I had messed up with my daughter Sophie, and I wasn't going to make the same mistake again.

I was there to see my son enter the world; things weren't so bad after all. Lauritia was beaming; Tommy was her firstborn. She's a fantastic mother, full of love for our son, Thomas Bertrand Kennedy V. It was then that I finally realised it was time to give all this drug dealing up for good. People kept ringing me for weed but I told them I was out of the game these days, and eventually my phone stopped ringing, when they found new dealers.

When Tommy came along, I decided I should get a car. I had been driving since I was 17 but had never passed my test; it was time to get this sorted. I paid for a week-long course up in Blackpool of all places and went there in the middle of winter. Blackpool was like a ghost town. By the end of the week I had passed my test. I came back with my brand-new driving licence, mission accomplished. I bought a car off a friend of mine who lived out near Willesden for a grand, sorted out the tax and insurance and parking permits, and for the first time in my life, I was legal, at long last.

'The road of excess leads to the palace of wisdom'
- William Blake

I sometimes wonder how lucky I am to be alive and still in one piece, for tomorrow is promised to no man.

My brother Anthony made his way back out to Dubai in 2008, setting up a window cleaning business. I admired his spirit. He wanted out of Warrington big time and wanted to try his luck in the UAE. It's not everyone's cup of tea, Dubai, he likes it out there though. After the last trip he had out there, he made his mind up to give it a go.

He studied Dubai, and because of the sheer number of windows and glass buildings, he decided he would set up a window cleaning business; his entrepreneurial mind was working overtime.

He left behind his wife Paula and the kids, determined to make a new life. He landed in Dubai with no idea how he was going to make it out there, just a will to do it. One thing at least, he could have a beer in Dubai, unlike in neighbouring country Saudi Arabia. Alcohol sale and consumption, though legal, is tightly regulated in Dubai. Adult non-Muslims can consume alcohol in licensed venues, typically within hotels, or at home with the possession of an alcohol licence. Places other than hotels, clubs, and specially designated areas are typically not permitted to sell alcohol.

Break For Love

In 2009, after being in the halfway house for two and a half years, I received a letter from Notting Hill Housing. They had found me a one-bedroom flat in North Kensington in the aptly named Sunbeam Crescent. I moved in, and Dandi helped me by painting the flat. Things were looking up at long last after many years: I had a place of my own to finally call home.

The Delinquents split up in 2009 after about 150 gigs. I think Steve let them go, to move forward; he was too old, they wanted a younger singer, fair play to him. Edd wanted to start a new band and quickly found a young singer from Bristol called Whiplash, who worked behind the bar at the Portobello Gold. He had come to London with his friends Tim and George after travelling around the world. Whiplash is a natural-born entertainer, bristling with charisma, a great front man in the vein of Iggy Pop or Ozzy Osborne.

They set about rehearsing.

Steve put another band together with Neil, a great guitarist who ran the music shop on the All Saints Road, selling and repairing guitars. Neil was from Crewe and was well-known to musicians who lived around Portobello. They brought in Wiggsy on bass, Michael Giri on drums, all seasoned musicians, they had a great sound. Out of the ashes of the Delinquents rose two new bands, The Steve Dior Band, and Pink Cigar.

Sid Mayall had been to Ibiza earlier in the year and had seen the name 'Pink Cigar' on a bar out there. Pink Cigar was also a slang name for a man's penis. It suited them, they were a sexual rock and roll band. Young girls flock to their gigs. I have seen women mesmerised by them, a few jealous boyfriends, and disgruntled older musicians who can't stand them, but like all great bands, they divide opinion.

Every opportunity I had I would take Tommy out in his pram, change his nappies, feed him, play with him. He brought out a new dimension in me. Tommy and his mum lived in Neasden near the North Circular. Lauritia spent every minute with him for the first three years, she idolised him.

Another major tragedy happened. My best mate from Warrington, Rob Taylor, suddenly died. He was 49. He had caught pneumonia. I had seen him only three days before his death, and he was laughing and joking; he was off to India for six weeks. He gave me a massive bear hug on Portobello Road. I never saw him again. I was devastated.

We had been through so much, coming to London together, mates in Warrington from the age of 11 onwards. I loved Rob; he was an amazing character, full of life, with a deep love for his family. About ten of us had settled in London years before, and all of them left, went to Australia or back to Warrington. Now Rob had died I was the last man standing. He was cremated at Kensal

Rise Cemetery on Harrow Road. Hundreds turned up, old friends from Warrington, Jarv - a good friend, Al Whaley, Al Moye. The church was packed. Women were sobbing, it was as if Rudolph Valentino had died. Rob was great friends with lots of women.

Friends from all over Kensal Rise and Ladbroke Grove turned up, Paul Greendale, Vanessa Murphy, Rob's family, his daughters, his mum and dad. They draped his coffin with the Man City flag. I said goodbye to one of my best friends, who knew me better than most.

Robert Albert Taylor, AKA the Rat. See you again one day mucker, on the other side, gone but never forgotten. We all hit the pub and reminisced about him. I remembered when we went to Spain and I fell asleep in a crowded club with just my shorts on; I woke up half an hour later and everybody was pointing and laughing at me, Rob was cracking up with a big smile on his face, I looked down and I was starkers, he had pulled my shorts off and thrown them on the bar while I had been asleep. He would do anything for a laugh. I was bright red from the sun and the shame, and he had thought it was hilarious. I have a thousand memories of Rob; he was a real one off character who I will never forget. I left the pub hammered that night. His friends and family gave him a great send-off.

'I haven't failed. I've just found 10,000 ways that won't work'

- Thomas Edison

I was staying out of trouble. There were always financial problems, but I got by. I kept thinking I should write a book, but it had to be natural, I couldn't force it. The time feels right now, it is flowing out of me, the good, the bad, and the ugly.

Pink Cigar started doing gigs. The first one was in Great Portland Street in early 2009, and after that they were playing all over London in that first year. They gelled, and the live performances were electric, filled with women and people wanting to party. Pink Cigar gave it to them big time. It seemed they were always playing gigs, they were young, and the world was at their feet.

The Steve Dior Band started playing some low-key gigs around Ladbroke Grove. Steve wrote a whole new set of songs; he was in his element on stage with a brand-new band.

The Grove was awash with the news about the two bands. I was now managing both bands under ZodoA Management, a name I had picked up in Thailand when I was working with Mentona K.

I saw my son Tommy nearly every day. I loved his company. I started to take him out playing football after I met Mani in a London Casino one night and found out he was a football coach. We would turn up on a Saturday morning and for the next four years, Tommy played football. He became good but for some reason he became bored with it too; he was still incredibly young and still finding his feet. We took him to Morocco, Tunisia, and Spain, and he went regularly to Slovenia to see his grandparents.

He was going to one of the most multi-racial schools in the country, Brook Green. He learned about all cultures from all over the world. I like that. I didn't want him to grow up a racist. He got along with everybody; I am enormously proud of the way he carries himself. He is a very well-mannered young boy, wise beyond his years for sure, and he speaks and understands Slovenian.

Life carried on. I was again booking gigs for the Steve Dior Band.

Steve could still attract the women in his 50s; he looked like one of the Rolling Stones and he had a great stage presence.

His sisters Middi and Esther would come to the gigs, along with his mother Dianne. They all lived together in the Clearlake Hotel, which the family owned since 1968, right opposite Hyde Park, on Prince of Wales Terrace, Kensington. They also owned the block of flats next door. Steve was constantly writing and doing smack, but he was basically operating normally. A lot of people know Steve from the London Cowboys days, they were a big underground band in the 80s and achieved cult status. Steve was his own man and moved at his own pace, you couldn't rush him. He had been married in Los Angeles, and had two kids back there,

Jez and Scarlett; he would talk about them constantly. He missed them, but he was not in the right frame of mind to leave London then.

I also met Big Alan Clayton from the Dirty Strangers, who had just returned from a world tour with The Rolling Stones. Alan is great friends with the Stones guitarist Keith Richards, who had also played on the Dirty Strangers album. Alan lived with his wife Jacqui and son Paul in Shepherds Bush. We became friends. Alan was itching to play again, a fanatic QPR supporter, and a good man who always helps his friends out.

I was booking bands at the Paradise in Kensal Rise. I had them playing upstairs on a Sunday night for about six months, and we had some great gigs. There was a young band around then called The Skylarkers, fronted by Travis Franks, son of Tracy Franks. Harry, a young kid from Sunderland, was in the band with Travis. They had a great look and played numerous gigs, but after a while, they split up. I thought they should have carried on. One of the hardest things a band can do is stay together; sometimes there are too many egos in the band.

It started to happen with Pink Cigar. I wanted them to sign a management contract, but they decided they would go it alone. We parted friends and we wished each other well. I mean, they were like my babies and I had been through so much shit, but my spirit was strong and so was theirs.

When Acklam Village Market opened I met Dermott Cadogan and his wife Caroline, and we became good friends.

Dermott is a no-nonsense businessman; he and his wife Caroline made Acklam Village Market what it is today, a thriving business with bars, food stands, and live music. I did gigs there with them and it was fun. They open only on a Saturday and Sunday, and it's always packed. They also open the odd night in the summertime. It really is a great place to visit and brings character to Portobello.

In the summer months, Portobello is buzzing with thousands pouring down Portobello Road to visit the world-famous Portobello Market. The film *Notting Hill* was filmed around Portobello, with actor Hugh Grant and Welshman Rhys Ifrans, who later went on to make a film about Howard Marks, playing

Howard. The film *Notting Hill*, not really my cup of tea, brings thousands of tourists to get their photo taken with the blue door. It always amazes me why people would bother, years later.

When on Portobello Road I came across a young Manc, Caesar, who had been released from jail in Japan for smuggling. He was loud and funny, and we became friends. All kinds of characters frequent the venues and pubs around Portobello. Nicky and Sue, both in wheelchairs, were nice women who would come to the gigs and have fun, big fans of Pink Cigar and the Steve Dior Band.

Along with the rich people living in big houses, there are council estates surrounding the area and you would hear about the odd murder here and there, around North Kensington. But in general it's a great place to live.

Kensal Green was full of people who had found the rents too expensive around Notting Hill so moved there, just over the Harrow Road and near the canal. Kensal Green is an area in north-west London, in the London boroughs of Brent and Kensington and Chelsea. The surrounding areas are Harlesden to the west, Willesden to the north, Brondesbury and Queens Park to the east and Notting Hill and White City to the south. I first met Alan Blizzard in Harlesden at a gig and we clicked and became friends. Al was married with a few kids. He was a lover of music; he loved to sing and play guitar, and he had been in numerous bands over the years. He is now currently fronting a band called the Electrics. He is also a graphic designer, and helped me out with graphics. He never charged me; he was that kind of man, he did favours for friends. Harlesden had a reputation for being rough, but I liked it. Alan loved living there, he was always up for a laugh.

Harlesden is an area in the London Borough of Brent, northwest London. Its main focal point is the Jubilee Clock, which commemorates Queen Victoria's Golden Jubilee. Harlesden has been praised for its vibrant Caribbean culture and unofficially named London's reggae capital. The population includes people of Afro-Caribbean heritage most notably, as well as Irish, Portuguese, Brazilian, Somalis, with smaller Latin Americans and East Africa groups within the community.

Micky P was a promoter and a jazz singer who used to work in the West End and was putting on gigs locally in Ladbroke Grove. A few years later Micky went on to start the Portobello Live Festival. Micky was always buzzing around like he was on speed, even though he wasn't, that was just his character.

This was the press release:

Held over Sunday and Monday of the May Day Bank Holiday, Portobello Live! provides maximum accessibility for minimum spend. One affordable wristband allows entry to all Portobello Live! venues over two days. Under 16s go free. A great lineup of new and established bands and performers, rock royalty, superstar DJs, and special guests will perform at Portobello's iconic pubs, clubs, and venues. Portobello Live! partners include Rough Trade Records, Wall of Sound (25th anniversary), Notting Hill Carnival pioneer Leslie Palmer MBE, Great Brain Robbery (live talismanic blues), Blatantly Blunt (hip hop and grime) and The Roughler Club (spoken word). We are also proud to partner with J P McCormack's Portobello Vegan, whose market will be serving up delicious food and drink as well as ethical clothing, cruelty-free beauty products, and vegan artisan delights, and the Sustainability On Screen film festival, showcasing a compassionate and environmentally friendly lifestyle. Movies include the community sustainability-themed Down To Earth and environmental films.

Aimed at preserving West London's rich and diverse artistic heritage, the festival provides a deserved platform for the area's past and present music and cultural history. Venues are all within walking distance and include Subterania, Mau Mau, Rough Trade, Vinyl Café, Maxilla Social Club, the Muse Gallery and The Italian Job.

Director: Micky Pallant

Patrons: Don Letts, Anna Chancellor, Mick Jones, Kevin Allen, Chris Salewicz

I met Allister, who used to supply props for parties, Tony, the driver, a friend of Scouse Kenny, all kinds of writers, poets, musicians: you can meet anybody around Portobello Road.

I would, on occasion, meet somebody I had served time with in Jamaica, around Harlesden. It was a chilling reminder of how lucky I was to be back in England doing what I loved. I had travelled the world for over 12 years, and I loved it: travelling was in my blood. I loved being in London too. The world was here, every nationality you could think of. Travelling around London can at times be like travelling around the world, it helped satisfy my wanderlust.

Another tragedy shook the residents of Notting Hill when the grandson of Oswald Mosley, Alex Mosley, died of a heroin overdose in 2009. You would often see him around the Portobello Road. He had a restaurant on the fashionable Hereford Road and he was reputed to be a mathematical genius - but he had been using smack for 15 years. His house was only yards away from the former TV host Paula Yates, who had also died of an overdose in 2000; it just goes to show drugs can grab hold of anybody, rich man, poor man, beggar man, thief.

Gill, the mother of my daughter Sophie, suddenly died in 2010 at the age of 45. I was stunned when I heard the news. Myself and Gill had been good friends for over 25 years. I didn't go to the funeral because she was married at that time and I didn't want to cause any offence. It hit both of her daughters very hard. Sophie and Gemma and their mother Gill had been like the Three Musketeers growing up back in Warrington; she had been a great mother to both of them, and it must have been a massive blow to all her family.

A year later Sophie married a young man called Anthony, from Salford, and they set up home in Warrington. Sophie already had one child, Barclay, who was a bright boy, and they had two more children, Theodore and Penelope, and the family was complete. I was a grandfather and saw them very occasionally; they are loved and grew up to be lovely children. My daughter carried on working part-time at British Telecom. She is an awfully hard worker and provides for the children the way I never did when she was growing up.

Now, she is grown up with her own children. We do get on these last few years, better than we ever did when she was a kid.

They came to London a few times and we would meet up; I was always glad to see them.

You Name It, Dubai Has It, Or If It Doesn't Have It, It's Building It

I have been to Dubai a few times. It was fun; not sure about living there though. My brother was still living out there and he was doing well with his window cleaning business. He had people working for him and he was making money; he had turned his back on ringing the change. I went and stayed with him for a couple of weeks in the wintertime, when the sun was not so fierce. He knew everybody out there. We had fun; plenty of bars and clubs serving the oil-rich expats that worked there.

I would then fly on to Thailand after leaving Dubai, to see old friends down in Koh Samui. I couldn't believe how it was changing, from a sleepy tropical island in the 80s full of long-term travellers to… They now have McDonald's and thousands of package holiday travellers. That's progress I suppose.

When I arrived back at Heathrow four weeks later, I felt refreshed and ready for anything. Money was tight, but I was always having fun, which is the main thing in my life after family.

I also like East London, around Shoreditch, and the markets on Brick Lane. I was constantly travelling around London doing gigs, watching bands, and meeting friends.

The Rotten Hill Gang had been an ensemble of musicians started by Gary McPherson and Red West. Gary had played with Big Audio Dynamite. They used to rehearse in Mick Jones' studio in Acton. It was a great studio, very homely, and they would invite other musicians down to film The Rotten Hill Gang TV Show.

Red West was the lead singer, a young West Londoner who had style and panache. They would be joined on vocals by Hollie Cook, the daughter of Sex Pistols drummer Paul Cook, Annie Bea, a great singer from West London, Mallet Hallet on drums who had played with Wendy James and Transvision Vamp, and Gus Robertson on guitar who had played with Razorlight. A variety of musicians would play with them. Another great singer who sang with them was Alexia Coley whose family owned the Ripe Tomato on All Saints Road.

Don Letts was always around with his camera, and the writer Chris Salewicz who used to write for the *NME* and had written bios on Joe Strummer, Bob Marley, Mick, and Keith, and recently Jimmy Page.

Chris was always around the band; he was a great writer, and his son Cole was a singer in bands. The Rotten Hill Gang used to play at George Vjestica night, who was playing with Groove Armada at the time, a weekly night at the Pelican pub on All Saints Road.

Their music was a blend of hip hop and soul. They went on to perform all over, Glastonbury, Notting Hill Carnival, and toured with Big Audio Dynamite around the UK. Mick Jones would step up and play with them occasionally, unannounced of course. They supported Razorlight along with Pink Cigar in Powis Square for one year. It was like a big family.

Occasionally I would head back north to see my father. He would always urge me to stay out of trouble whilst I was there.

I would head out into the town centre to see old friends. Some were heavily involved in crime at the highest level, but that was no business of mine. We were still friends though, always had a laugh. Warrington is perfectly situated between Manchester and Liverpool, close to the motorway, and you could guarantee hundreds of kilos would be coming through daily. I had replaced my buzz of crime with music and that suited me.

I didn't want to spend any more time in jail. Fair play to the ones who were taking the risks, and big risks they were taking; if they were caught they'd be looking at big jail sentences, Risley, Walton, and Strangeways are full of them. I heard a mate of mine had just been jailed for 6 years, so we went up to see him in Altcourse in Liverpool. He was in good spirits; he knew he just had to grin and bear it. After the visit I was glad to get back in the car and get away from there: prisons give me the creeps these days.

My father seemed to be well. My brother and sister were not living near him and neither was I, but we all stayed in contact with him by telephone, the bond was strong. I would go and see my cousin Jack and his wife Claire and they always made me welcome; a good laugh would be had by all. I have a large family across the northwest and too many to visit them all. I have many memories of the town where I was born - some good and some bad. I do miss the northern sense of humour at times.

After a few days, it would be time to leave. I would jump in the car and make the 4-hour journey back to London usually nursing a massive hangover from the night before. It had been good to see the family and friends; arriving back in London ready to chase the next dream.

'Wealth is the ability to fully experience life'
- Henry David Thoreau

The following day after breakfast I took a walk on to Portobello Road. I ran into a friend of mine from Manchester, who lived in London, Caesar, who told me he had been locked out of his gaff on Lancaster Road a couple of nights ago. He was trying to get back in, but somebody rang the police, thinking that he was a burglar, and unfortunately for him, the police didn't believe he lived there. Deciding to check him out, they eventually got into his front door. They decided to take a look around the place, and they found 6 kilos of hash and £8,000 in cash, whereupon he was put into handcuffs and taken to Notting Hill Police Station. They kept him for a few days, charged him, then finally released him on bail.

He was fuming and was determined to get the best lawyer money could buy, to ease the prison sentence he knew would be coming his way.

He used to make me laugh, he had such a savage tongue on him at times, he could drive people away with his relentless venom; he was a classic of being his own worst enemy at times. He was one of those people, that you could never tell him anything, he knew it all. Still, he had his good side, he could be generous, and he did make me laugh. It was probably years of chasing up people who owed him money that brought out his unpleasant side. I have this thing about people, if the good points override the bad points, I can put up with them.

I had my own problems, didn't we all? As we make our way through the treacherous waters of life, nothing is easy, and usually, when things are going well, something or somebody would come along and fuck it up.

I think there must come a time in a man's life when he should go and live with his family on a desert island and forget about everything and everybody. Although Richard Branson is about the only one who can afford to do it.

Chasing Dreams and Planning Schemes

I started to hear about a band coming out of my hometown called Slydigs. My cousin Jack, who had been hanging around with Noel Gallagher before Oasis hit the big time, told me about them. I checked them out online and liked their songs. They were signed to Flicknife Records, run by Frenchman Marco Gloder, who had been around since the punk days.

I rang Dean Fairhurst, the lead singer, who lived in Burtonwood just outside Warrington. Dean was a smart boy and knew what he wanted, and we continued chatting for a few months. I booked three shows for them in London. They played at the Mau Mau Bar on Friday 6th September 2013 with the Dirty Strangers; the place was rammed. They supported Pink Cigar at the Fiddler's Elbow in Camden and played at Acklam Village Market for Dermott. They had great songs and were young and feisty.

I went up to see them at the Warrington Music Festival and offered them a three-year management contract. I also rang up David Morgan at the *Warrington Guardian* and gave him a story about Slydigs and how we met. All publicity is good publicity, right? The headline was 'They blew me away.' David ran the story the following week:

'The show was just in another dimension. Basically, they've got the looks, the attitude, and more importantly the songs to back it up. My cousin Jack Haughton introduced me to Slydigs' music so I decided to check them out for myself at their headline festival slot at Old Market Place in Warrington in July 2013.

Despite stage times running late and a shortened set, I did not leave disappointed.'

Slydigs front man Dean Fairhurst said: 'That night was a little rushed for us, but the crowd was great.' It's a two-way thing with an audience and we didn't have to work much to get them going. The reaction since then has been immense.'

Tommy Kennedy arranged a meeting and agreed to manage them. 'I can't believe my hometown has produced a band of this quality. They possess the essence of The Clash as a live act and the songs and finesse of The Rolling Stones. I've listened to their album constantly on repeat in my car. My initial plan was to get the band, whose single 'Electric Love' featured on Channel 4's *Fresh Meat*, to record new material at former Clash musician Mick Jones' studio in Acton.

'Slydigs have got something special. They've put the work in, their time is coming and I'm going to make sure they get the recognition they deserve.'

Little did I know what was in store.

The band had their lawyers look at the management contract, found all was satisfactory and then signed a few weeks later, and we set to work. Dean was sharp, and he had some good ideas, and we made a plan. My main aim at this stage was to get their name around London.

They came to London one weekend and they partied all over town. They came to Mick Jones' studio to watch a small festival organised in the car park outside the studios. Pink Cigar was on the bill and did a blinding set. Dean watched them with the rest of the band: Louis Menguy, on guitar and vocals, always polite; Peter Flemming on drums, and Ben on bass. Ben was a live wire, a plasterer by trade, and a handful on stage.

Tara Kennedy was with us, a good friend from the Notting Hill set who had drawn up the contract for me and the band. We all had a great time; the booze and drugs were flying about and we all spent the rest of the night partying at Tara's. I liked Tara, we were just friends, but she was always good fun to be around.

Pink Cigar had recorded an album, *We're Gonna Get You Out of Here*, at the studios near the All Saints Road. They still didn't have a manager, and I would see them around; we were all friends. Slydigs became my obsession. I promoted them relentlessly via social media, ringing record companies. I borrowed money from the bank and did everything I could to get them noticed. We organised a UK tour.

My father was not too well while this was going on. He had the onset of dementia. I was feeling the pressure; I was burning money on Slydigs. It's like feeding starving chicks, managing a band, they always want something and you're dealing with four different personalities all at once. Dean was the leader; the rest followed his orders. Dean could be on point when needed, Louis was easy going, and the women loved him, Peter was a great drummer and good fun, Ben was a laugh a minute. People were starting to take notice of Slydigs.

In the meantime, my son Tommy was growing up. He was five. I bought him a bike from a shop in Chiswick and watched him ride it. The very first time he had ridden a bike was on his fifth birthday – go on kid! He had friends from Morocco, Somalia, Afghanistan, Jamaica. He played with them at school and on the estate where he lives.

He is very sporty; I would love watching him play. I bought him boxing gloves and a punching bag. He loves his mother; she was doing a fantastic job with him. I tell him always to keep by his word, look people in the eye and give them a firm handshake, and always be polite. I know he was young; I was 48 years older than him, but I thought it's good to teach him young. I used to see him a lot before he started school. I would take him all over London in my car, blasting music. He had a good education musically, everything from Hank Williams to the Sex Pistols and more.

He must have thought I was mad when I turned up with Slydigs spray-painted on the side of my car. Perhaps I am, but I love things that are not normal; you only get one life. The best you can hope for with your kids when you are dead and gone is that they think Dad was okay. I tell him all the time that I love him.

It's hard: with my daughter Sophie, I wasn't around for her, but I still love her just as much in my own way.

My father was getting worse. I was travelling up and down to Warrington. My brother was still in Dubai. I loved my father.

Every time I got back to London, a few days later I would have to drive over 200 miles back to Warrington. I was in the middle of planning the tour, and I was spending money hand over fist. My father had to go into a home to be looked after, as his health was failing. I was working night and day for Slydigs, I was exhausted.

They moved my father to Warrington General Hospital. I rushed down to see him and spent a few days there, and I kept telling him he would get out soon. He looked at me and said 'Son, I won't.' My sister was there with her husband Pete.

My father was right. He died a few days later, the 24th of April 2014.

Tommy Kennedy III died at age 79. We came from nothing, but my father taught me manners. He told me not to go back on my word. I would miss our phone calls and his advice; he was a good man and he had conquered his demons. My mother had left him when he was 39, and he stayed and brought us up and never remarried. He could be a grumpy fucker, but he did like a laugh. I always stick up for my father, after all, he always stuck up for me.

We buried him in Warrington Cemetery, with his mother, his father, and my sister Donna who was my sister Lynn's twin.

We went to the local Irish club for the wake. My brother Anthony came for the funeral from Dubai. We got drunk and I even got on the mic and gave a speech and sang a song in his honour. He left behind his three children, his sister Val, and his brother Roy. He lives on through his family. I headed back to London, my brother flew to Dubai, and my sister went back to Fareham.

'It's amazing how much you learn if your intentions are truly earnest'

- Chuck Berry

Chapter Six

We mapped out a plan for Slydigs and their conquest of the UK music scene. They had shown faith in me by signing the contract. They played around Warrington for a while longer, then we set up a UK tour for May 2014.

We brought in a girl from Belgium, Jennifer Smitts. She worked for Warner's in Belgium and was a big fan of Slydigs. A bright girl, who spoke several languages and was shit-hot on the computer, she worked night and day for a year, relentlessly promoting and planning how to get them noticed. I take my hat off to her; myself and Lady J are both Librans and it was difficult to know what she was thinking, but boy she worked hard.

I put Slydigs with a good producer down in the Cotswolds, George Shilling. They spent 10 days down there recording their songs. He wasn't cheap, but he was good. I liked George. Slydigs had recorded their brand-new EP. The band was excited to be heading out on their UK tour. They were in London on the 10th of May and played the Spice of Life in Soho. Jennifer was there; she loved London and was a massive fan of Oasis. She moved from Belgium to London the following year. I introduced her to Rob who worked at Portobello Gold and he got her a job there.

Slydigs finished the tour at the end of May. There was a buzz going around about them, people talking about them. I hammered social media about them every day, putting their name in front of everybody. We sorted a gig out in Dubai with a guy called David Warren.

In the meantime, The Who's management wanted them; Trinifold Management had rung Dean and said to get rid of me and they would sign them up and put them on tour with The Who. They played the Ruby Lounge in Manchester; Paul Kramer came up from London to Manchester to see them. He worked for Trinifold, and the band fell in love with him when they realised what he could do for them. The writing was on the wall. I went to Dubai with them knowing we would part on our return. I had an airtight contract for another two years. Trinifold said they would walk away rather than give me a penny. Dean said he wanted me out of his hair, and he drew up a contract saying they would give me £5000 a year later, and £10,000 from any money they earned over £100,000. It would be good if they make it; deep down I didn't want to stop their chance of a shot at global domination, so I agreed. They did an arena tour of the UK, Canada, and America with The Who, and signed a three-year contract with Trinifold.

I wouldn't wish them any harm and I would love it if they do make it. I watched with interest from then on, willing Slydigs on.

David Morgan once again ran a story on them in the *Warrington Guardian*:

Warrington's Slydigs say they are 'astonished' after being invited to tour America with one of the world's biggest bands. The rock and roll four-piece will be supporting The Who at 14 arena shows in April and May as part of their 50th-anniversary celebrations.

Slydigs' opportunity came about after they impressed the iconic band while playing with them in the UK last year. Front man Dean Fairhurst also described it as a dream come true as The Who, along with the Beatles and the Rolling Stones, inspired him to become a musician when he was 13. By the same token, to support a band like The Who on possibly their last tour of America is astonishing and ultimately historic. 'We're very proud of what we have accomplished so far but for us, this opportunity is not something that we will be taking lightly.

'While we will enjoy every moment, we have a job to do, and when you're supporting a band like The Who you best be on your A-game. To have your name up in lights behind you gives you a boost of confidence. It can be rather stupefying if you think about it too long, but you have to just concentrate on the job at hand.'

Jack, my cousin, who was the tour manager of Slydigs, was still working with the band after we split. He got on well with all of them and they all lived close to each other. He was doing it out of a love for the band more than any financial game.

When Slydigs came to London supporting the Who at the O2 in Greenwich, I told our Jack to come and stay at a mine in London the night before the gig. When he arrived at Euston train station the next day I went and picked him up and brought him back to my flat. That night we went out and had a few beers and caught up on all the news. It was always good to see him; we used to buzz off each other, laughing and joking all night.

In the morning Jack made breakfast and we went down to Portobello, where he bought a few presents for his wife Claire, and the kids. The band would be sound checking around 6.30, at the O2, and he wanted to be there.

Around 5pm we both got in my car and hit the rush hour traffic. It took about 2 hours to reach Greenwich; he would have been better off going by tube, it would have been much faster. When we arrived, I dropped him off. He was on the guest list. He got out of the car and waved, said 'Cheers Tommy,' then was gone into the crowd who were making their way into the stadium.

I couldn't go. I would have felt a bit awkward with their new manager being there. I remember thinking as I looked back to the huge stadium, I should have been there, but best of luck to them, they are on the way upwards. I had played a small part. I started the car up and got about 50 yards then the car broke down.

I couldn't believe it. I spent the next hour in the carpark waiting for the RAC to turn up while the band was playing inside the stadium - I had to laugh to myself. Finally, the RAC turned up, and the guy fixed the car, it was only a small job. I thanked him and started the car up and made my way back to West London with a tinge of sadness.

'If you want to know who your friends are get yourself a jail sentence'
- Charles Bukowski

My mate Caesar was sentenced to 18 months for possession of 6 kilos, and the cash, at Isleworth Crown Court. He was sent to the scrubs, HM Prison Wormwood Scrubs, which is a Category B men's prison located in the White City area of the London Borough of Hammersmith and Fulham, in West London.

I went along to see him on a visit a few weeks later. He was in good spirits; he had been expecting 5 years and could possibly be out on a tag in 6 months. I know what it is like to be banged up, so I was sure he would appreciate a visit. I used to send him magazines and newspapers, from a local shop up for the road from the scrubs; they would deliver them daily. He came from a good family up north, and his parents were devastated, and quite elderly at the time, so I felt I should go and visit and relay messages back to his mum and dad. It was the least I could do.

I was always relieved to get out of the prison gates after each visit though, I wouldn't put my dog in there. Sure enough, 6 months later Caesar was released from Wormwood Scrubs on a tag. Wearing an electronic tag is most often a community service condition. As a rule, tagging a criminal is a condition of an early release from prison. The base unit is usually installed at your home. The court or prison order determines the exact location for the base unit.

Still, he was happy to be going home and went back to live with his parents, perhaps to build his empire at a later stage, who knows.

Sid the drummer with Pink Cigar lost his father, comedian and actor Rik Mayall, who died aged 56. He played the anarchist Rik in *The Young Ones* with his friend Adrian Edmondson. It was my all-time favourite comedy show. Rik died at his home in Richmond-upon-Thames, London, from a sudden heart attack after jogging.

His funeral took place on 19 June 2014 in St. George's Church in Dittisham, Devon. Among those who attended were Dawn French, Jennifer Saunders, Peter Richardson, Alan Rickman, and Mayall's *Young Ones* co-stars Adrian Edmondson, Nigel Planer and Alexei Sayle, and *Young Ones* co-writer Ben Elton. Edmondson also served as a pallbearer. His body was buried on his family farm in Devon.

It was a sad day for his many fans, but at the end of the day it was Sid's dad, so I left him and his family to grieve in their own way. Rik had always been a gentleman to me, and I could only imagine how the family felt.

Months later I bumped into Debbie Walker, who used to work for Island Records. She was doing PR for Pink Cigar, surprise, surprise. It wasn't long before Pink Cigar had signed a contract with me, and we were back together like I had never been gone. This was Christmas 2014, and I sorted a gig for January 2015, for London fashion week, for the rock and roll tailor Sir Tom Baker.

Irish Phil, who used to dress up as a woman in his spare time, would help out sometimes, picking Sid up at his home in Barnes, to get the drum kit in the boot of his car; he usually had a spliff in his mouth as he drove us around London, and his driving could be erratic. He very rarely charged me though, so we would put up with it.

Debbie got behind the band and did their press and Bio:

PINKCIGAR

Three boys from London and a force of nature from Bristol formed on the famous streets of Ladbroke Grove, London. Singing about the struggles and joys of trying to get where you want to be in life in London, it could be about a million other cities and a million other people. After releasing their debut album *We're Gonna Get You Out of Here* the band has extensively toured the UK, Europe, gaining momentum and earning their reputation as the biggest baddest live show in town.

The songs, the attitude, the excitement, the look, the fun, the aggression, the energy, and the fact they really mean it and live it. It's something that people can believe in and have a really great time at their shows. Pink Cigar is back with some new material gearing up for their new album which they promise to eclipse their much loved *We're Gonna Get You Out of Here*.

Band members:
Whiplash Jackson (Vocals)
Edd Whyte (Guitars/ Vocals)

106

Sam Rutland (Bass/ Vocals)
Sid Mayall (Drums)

On the night of the gig at the 100 Club a great friend who I'd not seen for 20 or 30 years turned up, Malcolm Lawless AKA 'Tank'. I couldn't believe it. I had known him since I was about 12 years old. He was a smart man and had an IQ of 145. He dressed like a biker; he had been a rebel his whole life. He was lawless by name and by nature, we used to joke. Malcolm had turned his life around; he had been a hardcore junkie and a prolific conman. He was a legend in Warrington. 14 years previously he had moved to Bury St Edmunds, started building trikes, got off the smack and the crack and started using his head. He'd given up drinking in his twenties and only smoked weed. He loved driving. He was like a human sat nav. He was a real good man of the very highest order.

We both looked around at the crowd; they were all surging forward to get a look at Pink Cigar, who were all primed and ready to play. I wondered if they would play 'Tommy', the song they had written about me a few years ago.

Whiplash, the front man, let rip with a huge scream before singing 'London Town Blues'. All the girls were dancing and ravishing him with their eyes, he had that effect on them. The band were on form this evening and the crowd at the 100 Club were with them, all the way. Edd was jumping around on the stage, giving the crowd what they wanted, loud rock and roll on his guitar. Sam, the bass player, was banging out the beats in time to Sid - soaked in sweat on the drums. It was a short and exhilarating set of 30 minutes and the crowd was going apeshit screaming more – more. Whiplash blew kisses to them all, then they tore into 'Hotdog by the River'; a fast and electric ride was given to the crowd. It was good to be back with Pink Cigar. They have got great chemistry on-stage; off-stage could be a different story sometimes as Whiplash and Edd could clash a lot at times, but I think that's what made them so good on-stage.

After the gig, we all had a few beers then I slipped away and left them surrounded by women. It would go on all night and things would get messy, as I knew from many previous gigs.

I headed out the door and onto Oxford Street. I went in search of my car, found it on a side street, got in and stuck the Pink Cigar album on, and drove home feeling good whilst soaking up the energy coming through the speakers at me. The Pink Cigar gig had been rammed, 300 people in the 100 Club on Oxford Street; it was a good start to the New Year of 2015.

I used to see Gary McPherson and Mick Jones a lot around Portobello Road. I asked Gary if we could use Mick's studio to record Pink Cigar's latest EP. He agreed that we could at some point that year. In the meantime, we were working out a plan for Pink Cigar at Debbie's flat. She was a good woman; she had worked for Island Records for many years and knew everything about PR.

Pink Cigar had by now been playing for a few years. 'Whiplash Jackson' was a ferocious front man. He was theatrical on stage and gave the audience what they wanted. He was a mad man on stage, uninhibited, up for anything. Edd Whyte was the leader or the motivator of the band and he could be very self-critical. He was the lead guitarist and wrote a lot of the songs by himself. He was also the youngest in the band. Trying to get Edd out of bed before 12 noon was nigh on impossible. He lived alone in a small room in Tufnell Park and thought a lot. Sam Rutland on bass, he could have been a male model, easily, the women drooled over him. Sam was a good man, highly intelligent, and worked the stage well. Sid on drums was a solid man who knew his music inside out. Sid makes me laugh a lot. His girlfriend Nicole is from the Dominican Republic.

Pink Cigar, together on stage, are a force of nature. They play deep down bluesy rock and roll, unlike anything on the music scene right now in the UK.

When you're a musician you live in your own world. Creating music, writing songs, honing their trade, they are not great at promoting themselves because they are too busy doing many things. It doesn't look good if they are bigging themselves up. I was a manager and even though I never had an office, I had an enthusiasm for their music and would try anything to get them noticed. I believed in Pink Cigar so much; they truly were the real deal in my eyes.

Working with a band was fun, you went to places, and more to the point, you had a reason to go. I started booking gigs all over the country and the band just wanted to hit the road and be seen.

They started rehearsing in various studios around London. Pink Cigar were well known in London and they usually drew a large crowd in the city. Outside of London they were not as well known. So they put a dynamite show together and prepared to play outside of London.

Because they were all working, we usually booked gigs for Friday and Saturday nights. I would pick them up after work on Friday, and we would drive out to places like Southampton, Portsmouth, Warrington and Manchester, where they would play. I would bring them back on Sunday so they could start work on Monday. It's not easy being in a band, especially when money was tight; they all had to work in between doing gigs and rehearsals and a million other things.

The band was tight like a well-oiled machine, and up for anything. Occasionally in the summer they would take time off and do a 10-day tour of Germany; the band loved Germany and the Germans loved Pink Cigar. Playing in Europe the promoters look after the musicians and they would get paid well, with food and lodgings provided.

The boys would come back from their tours completely shattered. As much fun as they were having it was still hard work, and they partied hard when out on the road, which took its toll. Whiplash worked behind the bars in London and on the building sites - whatever he had to do to survive. He lived in North London.

Sid, the drummer, did bar work too. He lived in a flat at the back of his parents' house in Barnes. Sam the bass player worked at a school and rented a flat in Mornington Crescent. He must have been really tired some Monday mornings when he turned up at the school.

Edd did bar work but he loved being out on the road gigging, and touring was his true love. Rents are so expensive in London; most of the time after they had paid out, they would be pretty skint and not have much money left, so if anybody offered them a drink at gigs it was well received. I have so many happy memories of working with them; we all had a purpose in life.

'If you lose your sense of humour you may as well blow your brains out'
- Lemmy Kilmister, Motorhead

Mau Mau Bar

I had by now been doing gigs at the Mau Mau Bar a lot over the years. The first one had been back in April 2004. The new owner, who had taken over in 2012, was from Northern Japan, Jay Hirano. We had got to know each other briefly from a gig I did the year before.

I liked Jay a lot. He had come to Portobello Road on his own and taken over the Mau Mau Bar which was predominantly at that time a Jamaican bar playing reggae, funk, and jazz. Jay was 29, and he was a second dan black belt in judo. He was training to be a stuntman, and was also a great drummer.

He was straight to the point and worked very hard. He had two doormen working for him, Dexter from Jamaica, and Rudi from the Dominican Republic, both huge guys. He had some good bar staff, Coco from New Zealand, Matt Bicknell, a young guy who had worked on and off at the Mau Mau for years and Jelone from the States.

The place was virtually jumping every night. It suited me, I prefer live music and DJs than just sitting in a pub. I've seen a lot of great bands there over the years and have never had any trouble. I arranged to do a Pink Cigar gig on a Wednesday night a few months ahead, we struck a deal and it went in the diary.

The Mau Mau was a great night, great looking women coming from all over London, as well as a mixed bunch of locals. KJ was always in there, a bit of a lady's man. Bullet ran the reggae nights on a Sunday for years, and he also used to teach the kids how to skateboard under the Westway. He was a brilliant drummer.

Jazz Refreshed on a Thursday was packed out and had been running for a long time. I even saw Liam Gallagher in there once. He said, 'I love this bar.' Anybody could walk through the door, on the Portobello Road; everybody came to Notting Hill at some point to check the place out. Micky P the promoter came in there often, along with many other promoters, talent spotting.

Scouse Kenny was boarding at Theresa's now. Theresa was Rob Taylor's ex-wife and she lived in a tower block. I had known Theresa since she was 19, and I used to go out with her sister Veronica. Theresa was fun, she'd known me for a long time.

Kenny was always working every night. He would have a few bevies around the local pubs on Portobello Road. He'd helped me out loads over the years. I considered Kenny a good friend. He loved his kids who were back in Liverpool; he was a Liverpool fanatic and loved gambling at the local bookies. He was a very stubborn man at times. I would see him often for a quick pint; he used to call me 'Rock on Tommy'! I could never get Kenny to come to any of my gigs, but I didn't mind.

We started plotting again for Pink Cigar; I was back on the merry-go-round. I started to think about America, as it would be a great place for Pink Cigar, especially Los Angeles. You needed a car to get around to gigs in LA though, and I had one major problem, I wasn't allowed back into the States for 20 years after being deported in 2003 for the drug smuggling conviction in Jamaica. Shit, none of the boys could drive, and we had to fund it all ourselves. I was racking my brains for weeks for how we would get around this, and then I had a light bulb moment.

New York, the Big Apple - we had friends there. They could stay in New York and ride the subways to gigs. It wasn't the best, but it was better than nothing, and America needs to see Pink Cigar. I contacted Anne Husick and Justyna Wozniak, a Polish girl who had lived in New York for 30 years, a friend of the band. She loved them. We arranged seven gigs around the Tri-state, New York, and New Jersey for the end of the year, which was 10 months away.

I wanted Pink Cigar to play at the Glastonbury Festival. I applied to all my contacts but to no avail; Glastonbury is virtually a closed shop, and unless you know somebody it is nigh on impossible to play there. I was disappointed but pushed it to the back of my mind.

I loved taking my son Tommy out. At every opportunity, I would get the boxing gloves out and encourage him to have a mess around with the bags. He was six now. I spoke to some of the clubs around London and they said to wait until he was eight. He was losing interest in football, much like myself. I loved playing football but watching it did nothing for me. Although I had seen George Best and Bobby Charlton play for Manchester United at Old Trafford when I was a kid, if I was to support a team it would have to be Manchester City in honour of my mate Rob.

George Best used to live on Oakley Street, in Chelsea, off the King's Road, I met him a few times when I lived there in '84. He was a nice man and used to drink in J Henry Beans on the King's Road. I also met him in Australia, and he laughed and said, 'What are you doing here?' Life was good, Tommy was getting well looked after, things were ticking along nicely with Pink Cigar, and I was having fun. What more could a man want?

We thought about hiring a tank and driving it around central London blaring away Pink Cigar music outside the *NME* offices and radio stations, with Pink Cigar standing on top. Edd rang up a place that hired tanks and they wanted £4000 a day. I looked at my finances and shelved the idea, perhaps for the future.

Whiplash was useless with money; he would blow all his money buying everyone a drink and be skint the rest of the week. Luckily, he acquired a girlfriend, Carlotta from Italy, who kept him out of trouble most times. He really was a unique character, I liked him.

There were times he was on his shift working behind the bar at the Portobello Gold, and lots of women would come in; they loved the way he entertained himself and the punters behind the bar. He was a flirt and a bit of a lady's man until Carlotta reined him in.

Portobello Road is a hotbed of gossip, everybody knows everybody, and you can guarantee walking down the market you would stop and chat every five minutes with someone you knew, and they would fill you in on the news about whoever. I liked it if they were talking about the band. I used to start rumours about the band and see how it would fly!

Steve Dior was becoming a recluse again; not much was happening. Oh well, I knew he would surface at some point when he was ready.

I really was meeting loads of interesting characters. I like people. The beggars would always be tapping me up, they knew I was a soft touch, if they caught me in the right mood that is.

Tank started to come to London on his three-wheeled trike. We had so much to talk about; he really was a smart guy and his advice was invaluable. When Pink Cigar was touring, he would often help. He knew the roads all over the UK and used to do it just for a laugh. Around this time, I spray-painted 'Pink Cigar' on both sides of my car, in shocking pink; it looked mad. People were taking the piss, but I didn't mind, it was free advertising!

I met a new band from the Grove called Smiley and the Underclass. They were great, doing dub punk. My Japanese friend was the drummer, Smiley, from Eastbourne, the lead singer, James who used to play with Bad Manners was a great guitarist, and Ryan was on bass, later replaced by Derek from Mauritius. They were a mad looking bunch on stage but played great music, and more importantly had good songs. I wasn't managing them but sometimes I gave advice. Fuck it, I spray printed their name on my car too, in reggae colours!

I went around all the record companies, I was ringing the *NME*, chasing leads, anything I could do to get Pink Cigar noticed. Then an old friend of mine, Bucky, the American poet and songwriter who lived in the Grove, introduced me to Tony McKay. Tony was independently wealthy, had grown up in a castle in Scotland Inchcape. He had been adopted, his grandfather started P&O Ferries, and they were a fabulously rich family. Tony was a filmmaker and a property developer, loved reading books, and loved music.

Tony helped me out a lot. Not everybody understood Tony; he could be very blunt and eccentric, as rich people tend to be, but he seemed to like me, and he used to make me laugh. He had a passion for poker. I was constantly having to watch my money and Tony would help me out when he thought I needed it. He drove a top BMW. He liked the nice things in life. I like having a wide range of friends, you learn things from each other. Tony would often ask about Pink Cigar, and I started to think he might be interested in investing in them. We spoke for months about it, and finally Tony said he would set up a record company. True to his word, he set up Mad Tone Records and offered us £10,000 initially to record the album. The band was happy.

We were due to fly to Germany. My friend from Thailand, Rike, who had set me on this path all those years before, was doing a festival called Tropen Tango in her village of Wollmerschied. The setting was magnificent and reminded me of a miniature Woodstock. We arrived in Germany and we were going to stay five days in a field. We were treated like royalty, and it was great to see Rike after all these years. It was a great place too. We had a laugh, Whiplash was in his element, and Edd, Sid, and Sam were excited about the gig.

Finally, on the third day, they took to the stage. It was in a packed tent and was mind-blowing. The band tore into a blistering set and the crowd went wild; the band was carried off the stage like gladiators. Subsequently, they have been back to Germany many times, and have done some serious touring, and even made the German rock and metal charts. After five days we said our goodbyes and flew back to London.

Tony deposited £10,000 into the bank, and the band were ready to start recording in Mick Jones's studio in Acton. Gary McPherson was always in the studios. They were having a very creative period. Edd was singing on one of the tracks along with Whiplash, but when Tony got wind of this, he went ballistic: 'I only want ONE singer, that will be Whiplash! I don't want the guitar player singing it's too fucking confusing!'

I told Edd, 'You're not allowed to sing.' Well, Edd wasn't having any of it, and Tony brought his lawyers in; he was going to sue the band and he fell out with me, big time. Edd got his lawyers involved too. It isn't always easy being the middleman, as I have found out on many previous occasions. This went on for many months; it really didn't help with the recording process, and it ended our friendship with Mad Tone Records. I felt bad, Tony had been a good friend to me, but I had to side with the band. Finally, we gave the £10,000 back to Tony who said he was still going to sue the band.

Tony sold a few of his properties, bought a boat, and said he was going to sail around the world but would never forget how we'd let him down. I was shackled to my purpose. I wasn't going anywhere.

'Hark, now hear the sailors cry, smell the sea, and feel the sky, let your soul and spirit fly into the mystic
                    - Van Morrison

A few nights later I went to a gig in Camden to see some bands. The place was rammed and it was buzzing and there was a young band playing that night called The Garage Flowers who had been making a name for themselves on the underground toilet scene in London. Live venues were closing all over: the smoking ban, expensive beers, and greedy property developers all had a hand in the demise of many venues across the capital.

I had heard about the Garage Flowers from the boys in Pink Cigar; they were from Bristol, based in London, like Whiplash, who used to hang with them, along with Edd. I headed to the bar and ordered a couple of beers after getting through the throng heaving with people. I came back and Edd was gone. He must have gone into the back room where the bands were playing, so I went through, paid my fiver to the girl on the door and went searching for Edd. The back room was packed with women of all ages; there seemed to be more women than men, which was a good sign.

You could feel the excitement in the room and there was a feeling of anticipation. The support band came on. They looked like they had just stepped off a building site, the songs were terrible and the guitar playing was making my ears ring and I wondered if it was such a good idea to be here in the first place. Mercifully they finished after 30 minutes. I found Edd, and gave him his drink, and he told me he had been backstage with the band and they would be on in 15 minutes. Then he left me clutching his drink and disappeared into the crowd.

I was checking out the punters in the dark. I heard everybody clapping and looked towards the stage and thought this must be the The Garage Flowers: four young guys all dressed like rock stars. The lead singer looked like he was in the mood to rock, and I noticed the girls and women in the crowd all surged forward and left some of their boyfriends staring angrily at the band, which made me laugh. It was like being at a Pink Cigar gig.

It's always a bit strange when a band you have not seen before play songs you have never heard; it takes time to decide if you like them. They started playing, and the music drew me in immediately. They got the crowd on their side, the drummer was making time on the drums and the bass player was jumping around on the stage, and the guitar player looked like he was truly loving what he was doing, but nearly all the eyes in the room were on the front man: he was a superb performer with a powerful rock voice, knew how to capture a room and I could tell the women were mesmerised by his onstage presence.

They all had long hair and they looked good together. I could tell they had been playing together a long time as the chemistry and the musicianship were excellent. They tore into a blistering set, and the songs just jumped out at me - always a good sign if you can remember the songs - they gave a truly memorable performance and when they finished their set I was well and truly hooked by them, and their music.

The crowd had gone nuts. I noticed some women were lifting their skirts to the lead singer and you could feel a huge sexual thing was going on between the band and the audience. Some of the older guys in the audience were squirming at their girlfriends who took no notice of them, it seemed like they wanted to fuck the band there and then on the stage.

I made my way towards the exit. I never saw Edd as I went out the door. Soaked in sweat, I hailed a cab and went to a Chinese in Soho. I was ravenous and really didn't want to get involved in the after-party shenanigans. I thought it was good for Pink Cigar and the Garage Flowers to have a friendly rivalry.

Scouse Kenny

I got a phone call from my friend Theresa one night asking me to come over and see Kenny. I drove over, and when I saw Kenny, he didn't look good. I told him I would take him to St Mary's hospital

116

that night, but Kenny would have none of it. He told me to come back in the morning. He was very stubborn.

I remember once when Kenny went to work with a broken leg. He was a tough scouser, built like a jockey, a quiet shy man – unless he had a pint, he would open up then.

I came back in the morning. Kenny got out of his bed and he collapsed in my arms. I rang the ambulance, but by the time they arrived, he was unconscious and breathing strangely. They worked on him and stretchered him down to the ambulance, he died on his way to the hospital.

Ladbroke Grove would never be the same for me and many of his friends. Kenny was a legend, a small man with a massive heart that finally gave up on him. We had a gig at the Mau Mau a week later to video Pink Cigar's single 'Generation Next' which we dedicated to Kenny. The place was rammed, and from the stage, I raised a drink in memory of Kenny. I was gutted that such a good friend had gone.

A few weeks later he was buried in his home city of Liverpool. They drove his body around Liverpool football ground, Anfield, before he was laid to rest. His son Kenny Jnr, his daughter Lee-Anne, and Amanda gave him a great send-off. They really are salt of the earth people, very down to earth and hospitable.

I drove down there with Theresa, her daughter Rubi and some friends from the Grove, travelling by minibus, BT John, Tony, and Les, a couple of brothers, Kenny's best mate Geordie, Jimmy, Lenny – loads of people came to pay their respects. Bubbles and Ronnie were on holiday in Spain, but they were there in spirit.

I have been to so many funerals in my life. I know we will all be the stars of our own funerals one day. Make the most of life, treat it as an adventure, and fill it with love for your friends and family.

Steve Dior flew to Mexico and checked himself into rehab. I wished him all the luck in the world.

I was meeting loads of great bands, like Santa Semeli and the Monks made up of Semeli, a Greek-Cypriot, amazing on vocals and singing with her sidekick from Iceland, Haraldur. I thought about managing them but Semeli and I clashed at that time. She was smart and highly creative and knew what she wanted. I remembered she was a Taurus, like my daughter Sophie; you do not get on the wrong side of a Taurus.

Joseph Dean Osgood had a great voice, like Rod Stewart. A bit wild when he was on one, still a great performer though, and we became good friends over the years.

Alan Wass was friends with Pete Doherty from The Libertines. Alan was great in his own right and he had a song 'Golden Heartache', which I loved. He had a beautiful American wife, Eliza; they were a great couple and we became great friends. The Freak Elite with Neil Anderson, Michael Giri, James Simmins, Wiggsy, they also backed the Steve Dior band. Taurus Trakker, Martin Muscat, a cousin of Mick Jones and his girlfriend Allison Philips, a great band.

The Dirty Strangers with big Alan Clayton played some great gigs around the Grove, and they even played the Albert Hall. They were managed by Ian Grant from Track Records. Alan's Son, Paul Clayton, manages them now. Alan's wife Jacqui, a very tight family, close and are great friends.

The first Portobello Live happened to be the brainchild of the local promoter, the legendary Micky P. He had great energy and he got things done. I ran a couple of the stages for Portobello Live at the Elgin and the Mau Mau Bar. Loads of young bands came, The Garage Flowers, Healthy Junkies, all girl band 'The Kut' who are making waves now, Whalls, a great four-piece from Kensal Rise. Bands from all over London played, and I brought a great young band from my hometown of Warrington, Serratone, all 17-year-olds, playing great rock and roll. Mickey brought in Dreadzone and The Rotten Hill Gang. The Cow pub was involved, Acklam Village ran by my good friend Dermott Cadogan, a good man, and a great friend, The Subterania, and anywhere that had a stage Mickey had a show going on. It was a great success and great for West London too. Well done Mickey!

The years were flying by. I kept thinking of writing a book, but I was so busy touring with Pink Cigar and running gigs. Lauritia and I were drifting apart. I loved her dearly but my obsession with music was all-consuming.

A good friend of Sid's currently was Tony Evans from Watford. He and Tank used to drive Pink Cigar to gigs and festivals all over the country and Europe when I couldn't. The year was coming to an end, November 2015.

New York was calling for rockers Pink Cigar - but first, we had a gig in my hometown, Warrington. This was the second time we had played in Warrington. The band always had fun and we were playing with Serratone, a great young band from the town. Edd gave an interview in the local paper beforehand for my friend David Morgan.

From the *Warrington Guardian*:

Rockers Pink Cigar will soon be jetting off to New York to find their fame – but not before heading to Warrington. The London quartet, who combine glam rock and 70s punk influences, will be playing at the Mix Bar on the corner of Barb auld Street and St Austin's Lane on Friday.

They have a connection to the town as their manager Tommy Kennedy, who had worked with U2 and Madonna, grew up in Great Sankey.

Guitarist Edd Whyte said: 'Our manager Tommy has connections and friends there and they come down for it. And when we played there last time we had a really good laugh so we're really happy to come back. It's Pink Cigar's last UK tour date before going to New York at the end of November.

Edd, aged 25, added: 'It's extremely exciting because none of us have been before. I think our style of music would go down well in America and everyone's been telling us to go. It's even what Matt Sorum, one of the original drummers from Guns N' Roses, said to us at a party.

'Travelling is one of the best things about being in a band. You get to go to places you've never been to before and you get to see a different side of things than you probably would as a tourist.'

Following their debut album, *We're Gonna Get You Out of Here*, Pink Cigar has just recorded a three-song EP at former Clash guitarist Mick Jones' studio in Acton.

'I loved our first album, but I think this is a step up from that,' said Edd.

'We've been influenced by rock and roll of the 1960s and 1970s and what we're doing is taking the essence of that and making it relevant to our generation. Pink Cigar play at the Mix Bar with Serratone this Friday.

We played the gig, and all piled back to Dean Hills, house of the father of Joe, the lead singer of Serratone; they made us all welcome, things got messy, and a good time was had by all. We left in the morning for the drive back to London, promising to return.

I applied for an American Visa, they refused it. Tony Evans said he would act as tour manager for Pink Cigar in New York. I drove to Gatwick airport and dropped them off; they flew out on Norwegian airlines to the Big Apple, and all hell was let loose. Justyna met them in New York and the band just went on a wild party exploring everything New York had to offer. They were professional; they played all seven gigs booked around New York and New Jersey. They were playing to a different audience, and the New Yorkers lapped them up and they garnered a lot of fans. I was liaising daily with Justyna by phone, and she and Tony did an amazing job taking care of business in America. I was pissed off I wasn't there, but glad the boys were at last in America. I owe Tony and Justyna big time.

Golden Heartache

That year, sadly, Alan Wass died, of a heroin overdose. I was devastated. A great friend and musician had gone. He was only 33 years old. Friends from all over London attended his funeral; Pete Doherty sent his condolences. We all gathered at the KPH run by Vince Powers and mourned Alan in his favourite pub. His wife Eliza, Alan's sisters, his family, and his father had lost their brother and son, they will never get over it. His good friend Tony Rowe was in America and couldn't make it.

Vince Powers is a legend in the music business, and his company The Mean Fiddler. Subterania, previously Acklam Hall, was originally opened in 1989 by the Mean Fiddler with well-known artists such as the Red Hot Chili Peppers, Eminem, Foo Fighters, Paul Weller, Madonna, Pulp and Alanis Morissette all performing at the venue before it was sold in 2003. In 2018, the venue was relaunched. Owner Vince Power comments 'Portobello has always been a creative hub and I am delighted to bring live music to the fore again in the area. Covering a wide variety of live performances.'

I lost my driving licence not long after. I was just over the limit and was spotted in Golders Green behind the wheel. I ended up being banned from driving for 12 months. I had just been to see Alan's family. Oh well, I was still alive and had much to be thankful for. Don't take anything for granted in this life. God-Bless Alan.

I had no car, so I started riding everywhere on a pushbike in the winter of 2015. I decided to start running a weekly night. I went to my friend, Jay, and I asked him when his least busy night was. He said it was Monday night and I figured, 'Hell, why not?' and Mau Mau Mondays were born.

I had first met Jeff Moh in 2015. He was always taking photos at gigs in his trademark bandana and gold-rimmed shades. Jeff had left his native Borneo in the 70s and travelled and hitchhiked through Asia, India, Afghanistan, through Turkey into Europe, and he came to Notting Hill, living around High Street Kensington when he was 17. He had met a German girl and moved with her to Berlin for 20 years, so he spoke German and English fluently, and when they split, he came back to living in London. He was a true maverick; he had been a gold dealer and made a lot of money - until his business partner ripped him off to the tune of two million pounds. Jeff was left in the shit with nothing. He picked his camera up and kissed it and took up his passion for photography once again.

He knew everybody on the scene. He told me he had been trained by the Shaolin Monks in the art of Kung Fu; he was small and wiry, in his 50s, extremely fit and up for a laugh, and his favourite saying was 'Hello Bro.' Jeff loved rock 'n' roll music and travelled extensively around London snapping bands. He started bringing bands to the Mau Mau to play a set; he had a good ear for music and all the bands loved him.

We started Mau Mau Mondays and Jeff documented it all for the first year. It was a blast, hard work, but hundreds of bands had a stage to play. I met them all, The Electrics, Alan Blizzard, Dale Senior, Jenny Lane, The Steve Dior Band played every week for six months. Steve really helped get the night off the ground; it was a blast.

I was happy and having fun. Jay cut the drinks to £2.50 a bottle and it was free entry. All the locals were turning up to support, Irena Halder, Roxie, Johnno, the list went on.

Howard Marks died - two days before my son's eighth birthday.

Dennis Howard Marks (13 August 1945 – 10 April 2016) was a Welsh drug smuggler and author who achieved notoriety as an international cannabis smuggler through high-profile court cases. At his peak he claimed to have been smuggling consignments of the drug as large as 30 tons and was connected with groups as diverse as the CIA, the IRA, MI6, and the Mafia. He was eventually convicted by the American Drug Enforcement Administration and given a 25-year sentence to be served at Terre Haute; he was released in April 1995 after serving seven years. Though he had up to 43 aliases, he became known as 'Mr. Nice' after he bought a passport from convicted murderer Donald Nice. After his release from prison, he published a best-selling autobiography, *Mr. Nice*, and campaigned publicly for changes in drug legislation.

His daughter, Amber Marks, is a professor of Criminal Law at Queen Mary, University of London.

I couldn't believe it; he had lived a great life though. His family had a quiet funeral, and his mate Chris Sullivan, a fellow Welshman, and a writer who had run the legendary Wag Club for 17 years, held a memorial dinner upstairs at the Cow pub.

Loads of people came from across the UK, gangsters, actors, musicians. Rob Spragg from Alabama 3 sang; Suggs from Madness, Billy Idle was there, his old friend from Manchester who used to DJ at the Hacienda who still regularly DJs worldwide, and now hops back and forth between London, Manchester, and Ibiza to spin only at the best venues. Lee Harris, who had the head shop on Portobello. Many people had stories to tell about Howard. I was too shy to say anything.

Howard had done a lot for me. The last time I saw him was at the great train robber Ronnie Briggs' funeral. We drove Howard and his daughter Amber home across London afterward, laughing and joking all the way, with my mate Dandi driving. I've got fond memories of Howard.

Tommy was doing well at school. We started training him at the All-stars boxing club on the Harrow Road, West London. He took to it like a duck to water and loved the training.

Pink Cigar were playing all over the country, releasing new music, working hard, partying. London is just one huge playground, and if you're looking for fun it's all here. The band had girlfriends now; Sam the bass player had met Rosie. Edd was the only one who was single. He can be a bit morose at times, a perfectionist, but when you got to know him, he had a biting wit and was extremely ambitious. His father Michael was a filmmaker and had made a documentary on the Carmelite Monastery, just around the corner from where I lived, near St Charles Hospital. All the band are interesting people, they have spent years playing together.

The music industry has changed so much over the last 20 years. *The X-Factor* and all those shows are complete rubbish, people are being brainwashed. Where are all the characters in the media today? Who can we read about that is interesting? Well, I know: Pink Cigar, Smiley and the Underclass, The Rotten Hill Gang, Steve Dior - the list can go on - are waiting in the wings and you won't be disappointed.

One of the great London promoters is Mikey Johns from This Feeling. He puts great shows on. He works ridiculously hard, with guitar bands, and is friends with Noel Gallagher and Kasabian. We need these people to give rock and roll bands a stage. London is an exciting city; people complain, but I lap it up.

The Mau Mau Mondays were going well. I brought in DJs, like Dr. Philgood aka Phillip Mullet - he and his wife Dianne were great friends of mine, I nicknamed them Posh and Wrecks. Di grew up in Chelsea and lived the high life, a member of the Chelsea Arts Club; they are all well-known in West London. DJ Alex Pink, a huge guy who I had met at Alan Wass's funeral, a great DJ and musician, came to play regularly.

I kept trying to get Pink Cigar on at Glastonbury, but no chance, it was so frustrating. In the meantime, they were flying in and out of Germany having a whale of a time. My good friends Caffey St Luce, Ben Dodd, and Heather Ferguson from the Zine Magazine loved them and always supported Pink Cigar. You must have a friend in this game. It is the hardest business in the world. I had lost my house, my liberty, suffered a heart attack, lost girlfriends, and been bankrupt; still, I had friends and I have spirit and I was having fun.

My good friend from Birmingham, who I had met randomly outside the Duke of Wellington years before with his girlfriend Joanne, Mick, is a larger than life character; his father was from the Yemen. Mick travelled the world selling silver; he loved dance music and was a massive fan of The Clash. We got on like a house on fire, he made me laugh so much. We went to raves all over London. He was constantly travelling, and anytime he was in London we had a top laugh.

I never really think about my age. I have energy and I'm alive; I won't worry about the trivialities of life. I want, and I need, fun and adventure in my life.

Another good friend of mine was Ginti who lived in Shepherds Bush. She had travelled the world and had a heart of gold. She had led a remarkably interesting life and I would bump into her on the Portobello Road a lot when she was visiting her daughters in the area. She's a great woman and she should really write a book. Portobello Road is full of interesting characters. Ria, the Japanese art dealer, and her friend Sarb from Coventry were always great fun and loved Pink Cigar. All the market workers were great. Big Mark Jackson from Glossop was a graffiti artist, a poet, and a writer, a huge man.

Gaz Mayall, son of the blues legend John Mayall, had a band, The Trojans. Gaz ran a night in Soho, Gaz's Rocking Blues; it was running for over 30 years and is still going. Phoenix, the Egyptian photographer, a good man. Anne Windsor, the artist from

Liverpool. Damian, who ran the gallery, Allison and Sarah, great girls. Gregg Weir and Piers who ran the local Portobello Radio. Claire Howells, who had stalls selling vintage clothing. Graphic designer Suzie from Scotland. Ray Jones, the Welshman who had written a book and is in a band called Glory Bound. My mate John James from Grenada.

My friends are diverse, rich and poor, black and white, a great big melting pot we all call home.

'Some people never go crazy. What truly horrible lives they must lead'
- Charles Bukowski

The Businessman

In early 2016 I met Frank outside the Mau Mau Bar. I was trying to sell him cheap tobacco from China. I found out later we had a mutual friend, Fatty Molloy, the roadie with Primal Scream. It turned out Frank had been a tour manager and had worked on and off with Primal Scream for over 20 years before he set up his own business in the iron trade and had a yard out in Essex. Frank was from Romford; his family had sold flowers on the Columbia Road market in the East End for generations. Frank was a quiet man, never really said a lot but he had been around and had great stories when he opened up and told you. We started hanging around together, along with photographer Jeff Moh. We went all over London to gigs and parties. Both Frank and Jeff knew a lot of people. We had set up Notting Hill Promotions and started booking bands and having fun; that was the name of the game, nobody was going to get rich out of it.

We were having a top laugh. Frank knew London well. His grandfather had lived in Queensway and Frank had spent years coming to West London with his granddad. In his late 40s Frank split from his wife, and decided he wanted to live in Notting Hill where he had great memories from his childhood days spent with his grandparents on the streets of West London. Frank loved the reggae nights, run on Sundays by Bullet for over 10 years, a great night. Entrance on a Sunday was food that went to the local food banks, a great community spirit. An eclectic bunch all coming together, it's a great community vibe.

Patrizia the Italian girl was there. Life was sweet, or so I thought.

When you're a manager of a band it takes some very hard work; people outside the game think it's a doddle. We did a great night for Andy Cavendish in Tottenham one time. Andy is a grumpy fucker but straight to the point, he stands by his word and we got paid. Sid got stabbed in the back by a crazed crackhead the same night, after the gig, and was incredibly lucky not to lose his life. He spent the night in hospital; his family was worried sick, but he pulled through. They never caught the guy.

Sid is an extraordinarily strong kid mentally. When his father, the actor Rik Mayall, died, Sid became the man of the house, a big hole to fill. His father was larger than life in the house. Along with Rosie and sister Bonnie, the family had sold the house on Oxford Gardens and moved to Barnes, just over the bridge from Hammersmith. Thank God Sid survived. He works behind the bar when he is not drumming with Pink Cigar.

When I hear 'It's a Long Road to the Top' by AC/DC, I smile and have to agree. All kinds of characters latch onto a band. The women especially love Pink Cigar. A guy called Brian Boots fell in love with Edd. He was about 50 and scared Edd to death.

Their gigs were always attracting women of all ages from the boroughs of London and beyond. Famous people like Kate Moss and Sadie Frost knew about Pink Cigar. Pink Cigar are sex on legs, with their charisma, stage presence, and in-your-face bluesy rock and roll, they take no prisoners. Pink Cigar were like a precision machine, ready and waiting to play anywhere, anytime. They've played hundreds of gigs across London.

My good mate Malcolm Lawless was always in London; he would drive down from his home in Lakenheath near Bury St Edmunds. He had acquired a partner, Anne Emson, from Warrington, and they suited each other. Anne had seen the Rolling Stones when they had played in Warrington. Malcolm hated corporations and the greed they fuelled; he really was a rebel. He

126

hated money, he always spoke his mind, and he was very perceptive about people. A rough diamond, but a great friend to have by your side, and Pink Cigar loved him, they had fun on the road. He was a mine of information on things that mattered.

Malcolm and Annie came down for Carnival in the summer of 2016. Notting Hill Carnival is a sight to behold. They sure know how to throw a party in West London; the streets are alive with laughter and music. I love it. Frank, Brummie, Mick and I partied nonstop for two days. Jeff Moh took the photos. Portobello Gold was lively; the bar manager from Sweden, Helena Henning, had great taste in music, and her boyfriend Jem, from Wales, was good mates with Pink Cigar. Alex, Ewa and all the bar staff were up for having a laugh. The Royal Borough of Kensington and Chelsea was alive. The rich people fled their homes over the Carnival, they hated it. The rest of us loved it. Granted, there are a few robberies and stabbings, but the scale is minimal, and the streets are well policed and safe.

When I look back on my life, it's been littered with disasters and parties.

Jay was recording with Smiley and the Underclass and running the Mau Mau Bar. He was thriving; he had worked hard to keep the bar alive over the last four years since 2012, and we all appreciated that. He introduced me to his friend Emilie; she was a bright girl who used to do the sound at Mau Mau sometimes, a great girl, and we became friends.

Granted, when I was younger, I did some mad things, but I have three rules with my friends: no ripping them off, no trying it on with their women, and never grassing my mates to the police. I have learned some people really don't give a fuck.

When we used to go up to Warrington with Pink Cigar when they played there, I would see old mates. Nick Murphy was running a pub, a great character. Lloyd O'Malley, his uncle Walter was a mate of my dad, a former Mr. Universe, hard man. Mark Taylor, a mad northern soul man. Chris Lomax was training kids to box. Al Moye, a quiz king champion, knew everything. Dave Gleave from school days.

Warrington can be a bit like the Wild West at times; if you're looking for trouble you will get it. Friends of my brother

Paul and John Ruanne were a great crack, Tony McDermott used to go out with his sister Caroline. Brian Bedford, a good mate of my cousin Jack, all down to earth characters.

My mate Ainsley had gone to Australia 15 years ago. We connected on Facebook. Warrington is a tough working-class town with a great rugby team, the 'Wires' Warrington R.L.F.C.

Lee Daniels and his sister Sharon are great friends. I always have a laugh when I go north but I love London, it's been my home for most of my life now, but I would never forget my roots. Back in London, I was training twice a week with my son at the boxing club on the Harrow Road. Tommy is full of energy and has an inquisitive mind, and he would ask me about my life. I'm not proud of what I have done but my childhood was not easy. I don't want him to make the same mistakes I made; I want him to know I made mistakes but to know I have a good heart and I'm not a bad man, most of it was down to my sense of adventure and lack of control, but hey son, I'm still alive.

My daughter Sophie is all grown up and is sensible like her best friend Aveesha. I love both my children.

I started to get involved with Musicians Against Homelessness, which was started by Emma Rule and Alan McGee in 2016. Events went on all over the UK. I was the London 'Regional Manager', for a while, and went on television talking about the upcoming events.

Having been homeless and spent many years living in hostels, when I heard Emma Rule was looking for volunteers to put on events for the homeless I offered my services and started to get involved. It was a great success, thanks to Emma's hard work.

Emma Rule said in 2016 Musicians Against Homelessness had a twofold aim: to raise money for the homeless and to help young musicians to get gigs and exposure for their music.

The Harder You Work, The Luckier You Get

I was booking the acts for Portobello Live, running the Mau Mau Mondays and managing Pink Cigar. I had a heavy workload and hardly had a minute to myself, but I was loving it. 2017 was fast approaching; what a mad year it had been so far.

Tommy went to Slovenia regularly to see his grandparents. I liked that. He was learning about life, he could speak and understand Slovenian, and was broadening his horizons. He lived in one of the most cosmopolitan cities in the world, he travelled, and he had family all over the UK. He knew far more than I did at nine years of age. I genuinely believe you should bring your son up to be a better man than yourself, and we were doing the best job we could.

The knife crimes were becoming horrendous all across the UK. London seemed to be having the most knife deaths. In July of 2016 a young 16-year-old, Fola Orebiyi, was stabbed to death on Portobello Road over some trivial argument with a rival gang from one of the estates around North Kensington. Fola thought it was going to be a fistfight, but sadly not; one of the boys aged 15 and 16 brought a knife and viciously struck Fola in the neck and he fell to the ground and died an hour later.

A friend of mine, Claire, who ran a vintage market stall on Portobello, said her son was with Fola when the attack happened, and he had been traumatised and was moved out of the area for his own safety. My heart sank at the news. Claire asked me if we would do a fundraiser at the Mau Mau to help the mother of Fola with funeral costs, and of course I agreed.

We had the gig on a Monday night and a large crowd turned up. Claire was great and helped on the door taking donations, but still, it was a very sad occasion. In February 2017, his 15-year-old killer was jailed for 13 years at the Old Bailey. What a terrible waste of a young life.

In the early part of 2017, Jeff Moh and I parted company. He had found other opportunities. I wished him well.

Lauritia informed me she'd had enough of London and would be leaving town in six months, taking Tommy away from the estates in London where he grew up. I was heartbroken, but I had to accept it; my son was my main priority from now on.

I took him everywhere in London, to learn about his city, the museums, the parks, all over the 33 boroughs of London. I hired a photographer, a girl called Patricia Andre from Portugal who lives in London, a good friend of my mate, Billy Idle. She took some stunning photos of Tommy around London, a reminder for him when he's older. I am incredibly grateful to Patricia; the photos were amazing.

My daughter Sophie never got to see me while she was growing up, and I am terribly sorry for that. I spoke to her recently, and she said, 'You are an interesting man, but you weren't a great father.' She was right, but we're getting on and things are improving.

I had been living in Sunbeam Crescent for eight years, time was flying by. Frank had become a great friend and was looking for another business to start. He was becoming good friends with Jay from Mau Mau Bar too and in due course, Frank became partners with Jay and the Mau Mau Bar. Great news, it was a match made in heaven.

Not long after, a good friend Sally asked me to go to St Ives; her sister Lisa had died. It shocked me. Years before we had been great friends in St Ives, and on the beaches of Asia and Australia. Sally used to go to Nepal and buy cashmere to sell it on the Portobello Road markets around Christmastime. We had reconnected. Sally and I had been friends for 30 years; we'd had a brief but memorable time in St Ives. When she told me that Lisa had died it was hard to take in. I went down to St Ives with Frank, who had offered to drive me there. I saw old friends from my days in St Ives years before, like Nick Walmingsham, always great to see him and he had now acquired a girlfriend, Rebecca, and they were very happy. It was great to see.

We all attended the funeral. It was a sad day. Sally laid her beautiful sister to rest and we all got royally drunk in the Three Ferrets pub. We went back to London – life carried on.

One For The Road and One For No Reason At All

The Mau Mau Bar was getting even busier now Frank and Jay were partners. When Jay had taken over the Mau Mau Bar, he had built the stage at the back of the venue; the stage was made of wood and stood about 18 inches off the ground. It was a small stage that comfortably held a band and not much else. Behind the stage were long red velvet drapes that gave the place an air of sophistication. The Mau Mau Bar logos were hand made by a friend, Sandra Clarke from Wandsworth. They were circular and made of small yellow tiles that stood out, and they were hung on the walls.

Jay had built a long wooden bar with a silver chrome bar rail that gleamed and shone in the evenings. Frank, his business partner, had lights installed for the stage by a guy he knew who did the lighting for festivals. It was all controlled by switches behind the bar.

They had eventually installed air conditioning. The place was so hot in the summer and freezing in the winter time; the air conditioning turned into a heater in the winter so it was a dual purpose and worked really well, and the punters were very relieved when it was installed. On either side of the stage were the toilets, the ladies on the left, and the men on the right. It could be quite awkward going to the toilets when the bands were playing, because you passed by them in quite close proximity, and sometimes you would have to duck under one of the guitar players' guitar necks, but it also gave the place an atmosphere.

The toilets were ridiculously small; if more than 4 people were in there it would be crowded. There was a DJ booth built which fit snugly at the end of the bar. There were huge speakers in the four corners of the bar that served the ever-growing crowds that came regularly to dance and party.

The dance floor was quite small; the whole of the venue held 120 but I have seen it swell to 150, even to 200 people at a push, but you would be squeezed in like sardines. Because of constant complaints from the neighbours about sound levels, they finally had to soundproof the venue, at a considerable expense

Every bit of space was utilised to store the beer that was constantly in demand on busy nights. Jay would go to the warehouse in Acton each day for the stock and bring it back in his car, and stack it all by hand behind the bar. Frank had benches built in wood for the punters to sit on; they could be lifted up and the boxes of beers could be locked and placed in them. The entrance was painted yellow, with wooden doors with glass panels, and the red velvet drapes were behind the doors when you entered. It felt like you were coming in somewhere special.

Frank had bought a load of posters off one of the regulars that depicted rock and roll stars, all framed in wooden frames behind glass and adorned all across the walls; you would often see punters and tourists alike checking them out and taking photos. It all helped to give a good impression and created a great vibe.

Behind the bar, Jay had built a sign, so whoever was playing that evening, their names could be displayed up in lights.

The whole bar looked good in the evenings, creating a really cozy atmosphere for the bands and punters alike to enjoy. If anybody tried to cause trouble it would be stamped out very quickly by the doormen Rudy and Dexter who manned the doors. They knew all the locals and the troublemakers would be barred for life.

I was still bobbing and weaving, never knowing what was around the corner. Malcolm took Smiley and the Underclass on tour to Europe, but Jay the drummer couldn't go, his passport was with the Embassy. He was applying for full residency in the UK. I hoped he would get it.

Then some great news. Pink Cigar was going to Glastonbury, booked to play at the Unfair Ground Stage in the summer of 2017, and so were Smiley and the Underclass. Fantastic! Two great bands formed in Ladbroke Grove were going to play the biggest festival in the UK.

Glastonbury Festival (formally Glastonbury Festival of Contemporary Performing Arts) is a five-day festival of contemporary performing arts that takes place in Pilton, Somerset, in England. In addition to contemporary music, the festival hosts dance, comedy, theatre, circus, cabaret, and other arts. Leading pop and rock artists have headlined, alongside thousands of others appearing on smaller stages and performance areas. Films and albums recorded at Glastonbury have been released, and the festival receives extensive television and newspaper coverage. Glastonbury is now attended by around 200,000 people, requiring extensive infrastructure in terms of security, transport, water, and electricity supply. Many staff are volunteers, helping the festival to raise millions of pounds for charity organisations.

Regarded as a major event in British culture, the festival is inspired by the ethos of the hippie, counterculture, and free festival movements. It retains vestiges of these traditions, such as the Green Fields area, which includes sections known as the Green Futures and Healing Fields. After the 1970s, the festival took place almost every year and grew, with the number of attendees sometimes being swollen by gatecrashers. Michael Eavis hosted the first festival, then called Pilton Festival, after seeing an open-air Led Zeppelin concert at the 1970 Bath Festival of Blues and Progressive Music. The festival's record crowd is 300,000 people; this record was set at the 1994 festival when headliners the Levellers performed a set on The Pyramid Stage.

Glastonbury Festival was held intermittently from 1970 until 1981. Since then, it has been held every year, except for 'fallow years' taken mostly at five-year intervals, intended to give the land and the local population a break.

'Live every day as if it's a festival. Turn your life
into a celebration'
- Shri Radhe Maa

Grenfell

I woke up to the news that the block of flats near where I lived, Grenfell Towers, had set alight, and 72 people had died. I found out later this included my old friend Dennis Murphy from the Grove, and my Columbian friend Ramírez had lost his 12-year-old daughter. The community was in total shock. I raced down there on my pushbike to see if I could help. Up close it was haunting. There were thousands of people across the borough helping with food, clothing, and giving shelter.

Fundraising was held all over the borough to help the victims. Kensington and Chelsea Council had chosen cheap cladding that was placed around the building to make it less of an eyesore for the rich people who lived close by. This unforgivable act of cost-cutting had caused the building to be set alight. I see it every day when I walk past, and it still haunts the community, and will for decades to come.

I didn't want to go to Glastonbury, something I had dreamed of for years. It was terrible, so many people died. Children had been thrown out of windows by desperate parents who were caught in the inferno. My friends who had witnessed it wished they had never seen it, people were traumatised. Dermott opened up Acklam Village Market and thousands of boxes of clothing were brought in. The community of North Kensington came together, the spirit and generosity of the residents were fantastic.

Nothing will ever bring the victims back. A huge inquiry was put in place; it will take years and years. But the bottom line is, it was a terrible accident that would never have happened only for a cost-cutting exercise on the part of Kensington and Chelsea Council. The press was all over the aftermath for days afterward, from all over the world. People were walking around like zombies. Residents were heartbroken and angry at the same time.

What can I say? I love my community and the people from all over the world that live here. There is an amazing spirit and I feel like I was born here, this is where I am meant to be. I neither look up nor down at anybody, we are all the same, regardless of anything.

The days went by. I had to get Pink Cigar to Glastonbury, I needed to get them there by car, I had to snap out of it. I didn't really feel like going but I made my mind up I would drive them. Tickets to Glastonbury were £250 and it was impossible to get friends or family in. We drove down there in my Renault Clio which Frank's mate gave me after my driving ban was up.

I picked Sid up from Barnes, drove to Tufnell Park, picked Edd up, and then onto Archway for Whiplash and Sam the bass player. The band were in high spirits; Glastonbury is a great buzz, and to be playing there is something special.

Liam Gallagher was on the bill, and the Foo Fighters, but I didn't care, I just wanted to see Pink Cigar. We played on Thursday night and were the only band on in that field that night. The boys delivered a stunning performance and played for an hour.

There were thousands there, it was amazing. A tear rolled down my cheek, I was so proud, I knew what they had all gone through over the years to have the chance to play Glastonbury; it had taken years, but they finally got there.

We stayed for a few more days. It was Frank who had set it all up, he was well connected. Johnny Depp was there, and over 250,000 people; Glastonbury is an amazing sight to see, over 90 stages. I had last been there in 1993. I slept outside. The first night was freezing. I bumped into Sally from St Ives and stayed in her camper van. The highs and the lows of the music business.

Smiley and the Underclass played on Sunday, but I had left by then. I heard it was a brilliant set.

Chapter Seven

Tommy broke up for school in July. I was with him for two weeks, just me and him as he was leaving London in September in eight weeks' time. I picked him up from school and he stayed with me in London.

We had fun for a few days and then we decided to go north and see friends and family in Warrington. I wanted Tommy to know where his roots came from and to meet his big sister Sophie.

We drove out of London down the motorway, stopping for food along the way. We went and visited Paula, my brother's second wife, who has two kids, Mia and Alfie. Alfie was about 12 and a boxer, and he took Tommy to his boxing club, Hook and Jab, run by my old friends Derek Groarke and Chris Lomax. It was good to see them.

Tommy and Alfie had a good day. I wish my brother Anthony were there to see his son, but he was having trouble in Dubai and had had his passport confiscated. He had been unable to leave the country the last three years.

Tommy was meeting his northern family. I took Tommy around my old school, and showed him where I had grown up all those years before. We stayed with Claire, who had recently split from my cousin Jack, but they're still great friends and have a daughter, Cydney, the same age as Tommy. I went to see Anthony's first wife Cath, who he had two children with - Anthony Junior and Sarah - who both have children of their own. The Kennedys are getting much bigger.

My daughter Sophie was working so we arranged to meet her at the weekend. And finally, we all met; Sophie was 32 by now and had three beautiful kids, Barclay, Theo, and Penelope. We had a great day. I am immensely proud of her, she is clever and hardworking, bringing her kids up at the same time. Sophie's mum had died when she was 26 and I was her only parent.

I was still in Warrington when I got a phone call from Frank. He said, 'Malcolm is dead.'

My mate of 40 years had been killed on his trike four miles from his home. Malcolm was the best driver I knew. I put the phone down and I said to Claire, 'Can you take care of Tommy?'

My head was spinning; could this year get any worse? I drove to the town centre, parked up, and had a pint to calm myself down. Afterward, I sat for hours alone on the town centre benches, casting my mind back over the years, school days, rugby, parties, London. I just couldn't get my head around it all. Malcolm was dead, one of my oldest friends, so full of life. He had just been all over Europe on his bike. He had driven thousands of miles with Pink Cigar and Smiley and the Underclass, he had helped me in every possible way he could. I told myself at least he died on his bike, and he wouldn't have a long painful life in an old folks' home. I was trying to figure it all out in my mind when I started to well up. My brother Anthony's oldest daughter Jamie walked by and said, 'Are you okay Tommy?' I just said, 'I'm fine.' I wasn't, but I couldn't tell her about Malcolm, who she didn't know anyway.

Death is so final. Why are we here? What is the purpose? I had to compose myself. I went back to Claire's and played with Tommy. When the kids went to bed, Claire and I talked about Mal for hours. I thought about Anne, Mal's partner, who had been planning to do a three-month trip around Australia on his trike, visiting old friends, Ainsley White and Jo Devlin, living there. Anne was going to leave Warrington and move in with him in Lakenheath. Now she would be going there to bury him.

The next day I went around the town with Tommy. I had to keep myself busy, anything to keep my mind off the tragic event. After a few more days we left to go back to London. I posted my thoughts on Facebook and it all hit me that night. When we arrived back, I broke down crying in front of Tommy, I felt so fucking sad. I was always telling Tommy not to cry, and here I was, his father, crying in front of him. He was only nine years old and he put his arms around me. I told him 'Son, it's okay to cry when you have lost your best friend.' I will never forget that moment, and I am sure he will not either.

We are emotional people, the Kennedys, we drink, we fight, we love, and we care for our friends. I do like that saying I picked up on my travels: 'False friends are like autumn leaves, found everywhere. True friends are like diamonds, precious and very rare.' Malcolm Lawless, aka Tank, was a diamond, whom I was proud to have called my friend for over 40 years.

I had to take Tommy home to his mother at the end of the two weeks. He would be leaving London for good soon. I pushed that away from my mind for now.

A few weeks later we drove to Lakenheath, Edd from Pink Cigar, Sid, and Sam the bass player. Whiplash was working. We arrived at Malcolm's cottage, where there were all his friends and family, including his son Ryan; I met them all for the first time. Fifty to sixty of his motorbike friends turned up and we all headed to the church. Following his coffin for the final ride in the long black saloon, I could hear Hank Williams in my head singing, 'Six more miles to the graveyard.'

It was a moving sight, seeing all his friends following behind on their motorbikes. He deserved this send-off. Jay and Smiley from The Underclass had driven up from London to pay their respects. Friends from Warrington, Lloyd O'Malley, Crank, Ste Devlin who lived in Dubai and many others came. It was a beautiful sunny day. After Ryan had spoken about his father, his sister gave her thoughts. Then it was my turn to speak. I was nervous but that was my mate, and I told everybody my thoughts, it came from the heart. We headed to the wake at the nearby football ground in Bury St Edmunds. Sid, Edd and Sam had a gig that night and left shortly afterward to catch the train back to London. I stayed the night and slept in my car; I didn't want to put on anyone.

'I decided to devote my life to telling the story because I felt that that having survived, I owe something to the dead, and anyone who does not remember betrays them again'
- Elie Wiesel

The Pills Were So Good You Could Eat A Full English The Next Day

Tommy was leaving in a few weeks to start his new life in Portsmouth. I spent all my time going with him to boxing, taking him out, doing father and son things. It flew by. At the end of August Tommy left with his mother Lauritia for his new life. I felt gutted, this really was the shit year, 2017. I would be glad to get it over.

I was drinking quite a bit. It had been a tough year, but Pink Cigar were keeping me busy. We arranged a memorial gig for Malcolm at the end of October on a Monday night at the Mau Mau Bar. Pink Cigar gave a great show, and friends and family had a top night. I was happy, I know Malcolm would want that. Anne came from Warrington, Ryan his son came, and we partied and talked about the good times. I am easy-going, and I take whatever life throws at me; I'm a survivor and I really am lucky in my life when I think about it.

Frank and Jay were busy with the Mau Mau Bar. Pink Cigar was recording again and doing videos. Smiley and the Underclass had a tour the next year in Japan. I heard Jay had finally got his UK residency and I was made up for him. Life was good again; I started to feel things were finally on the up.

There was a gig planned for the Joe Strummer Foundation. The last London gig he did was for firemen with Mick Jones on the 11th November at the Maxilla Club, which was in the shadow of Grenfell Tower. I was excited. I rang my mate in Birmingham, Mick, to let him know; he loved the Clash. He said 'Get me a ticket' which I did. The whole of the music fraternity in West London was awaiting this gig.

Mick jumped the train from Birmingham and arrived at my gaff in Sunbeam Crescent. We had a few beers in the Pig and Whistle. I dropped some Hawaiian mushrooms, they always make me laugh; I was in the mood for fun. We met up with Frank, Phil, and Di and went to Maxilla. It was rammed solid. Everybody I knew was there. I was having a great night, I couldn't stop laughing, and the music was great. The Rotten Hill Gang took to the stage and were joined by Mick Jones. It was a superb show and raised thousands for the firemen. This was just what I needed: a great laugh, good music, and good friends. It was a night to remember and went down in the history of the locals in West London.

It was a freezing cold night outside, but we didn't care, we were having fun. I was talking to everyone that night, laughing my head off. You only live once. I met a girl called Ruth and gave her some mushrooms. It was a night to have fun. Frank and 'Brummie Mick' were loving it, Di and Phil danced all night, Micky P was there, all the characters I know were there. Finally, about 2am I headed home; I was ready for sleep. Mick stayed on the couch at mine.

The next day, Sunday 12th November, we woke up and decided to go for some Sunday roast. I left the electric fire on, so it would be warm later when I got back. It was so cold outside. We ended up on a pub crawl, with Frank coming out later and meeting us in the Portobello Star. We were having a good laugh talking about the gig the night before. Mick was due to leave for Birmingham that night, in a few hours, from Euston; we were on a roll, taking the piss out of each other, just enjoying the vibe. I was dropping more mushrooms and was in hysterics laughing.

So, on we went. Somehow, we ended up in the Ginstitute on Portobello Road. The drinks were flowing.

Mick, Frank, and I were getting more pissed after we left the Ginstitute. We headed over to the Mau Mau Bar and bumped into Jelone, the barman from the States. A musician and an unusual looking character with a solid style of his very own, he had been living in the Grove for years. Mick headed off to Euston to get his train back to Birmingham, we hugged, and Mick jumped in a cab.

Jelone was living in Wembley. It was late and freezing. We ended up going to the off licence to pick up some beers, then jumped a cab to mine. We got to mine and the room was like a sauna - I had left the electric fire on during the day; I opened the windows, put the music on and we all sat down and started chatting. I'm not sure what happened after that, but we must have all fallen asleep on our chairs oblivious to what was going to happen within a couple of hours.

Meanwhile, Mick got to Euston and had missed the last train back to Birmingham, so he ended up getting a taxi over to stay with his mate in Clapham. Mick was a colourful character, always up for a joke, and travelled frequently, India for Christmas, Ibiza in the summer, South America, Cuba, Mexico, buying silver and jewellery. He loved the dance music scene and would often be in London. Mick used the gym a lot, but when he was out, he was out on the campaign trail, 24 hours, 48-hour benders, no sleep, a real live wire.

I awoke and could hear voices. Jesus, the flat was on fire and filled with black smoke! I went looking for a bucket. Frank shouted: 'What are you doing?!' I said, 'Looking for water!' He said: 'We have to get out, it's too late for water!' I was still half asleep, and I was choking on smoke and stumbled to the door. I opened the door, went through and the wind slammed it shut, with a huge bang. I had no keys to get back in. Frank came out; he looked like Sooty with black smoke, and the door once again slammed shut. I had forgotten about Jelone. I could hear him shouting. Shit, the door was shut! Luckily, at that moment the police ran up the stairs, and with a battering ram broke the lock and opened the door. Jelone staggered out, and we all headed down the stairs. I was feeling shocked; it was like a bad dream.

It turned out the police had been on patrol around the estate where I live on Sunbeam Crescent and luckily spotted the black smoke and fire billowing out of my window. There were police cars and fire engines all outside. This was only a few months after Grenfell and five minutes up the road. In comparison, we were incredibly lucky.

We were all a bit discombobulated, to say the least.

We were taken by ambulance to the burns hospital, the Chelsea & Westminster in Fulham. We had all inhaled a terrific amount of smoke. Jelone had burns on his hands, and he also had asthma I found out later, not good. We were taken straight up to the intensive care ward; none of us looked good, and the doctor told me another five minutes and we would have been dead. I was feeling a bit out of it to tell you the truth, and I was also worried about all my things back at the flat. I had left everything, including my wallet, my keys, and my mobile. Funny, I was lucky to escape with my life but thinking about my things, at a time like this! I remember needles going in my arm and then nothing. Jelone was sedated, Frank was sedated.

I woke up 24 hours later covered in tubes. I really wasn't sure where I was and then it all came back to me. I looked around the ward and I saw there were two policemen sitting in the ward; I wondered why they were there. I had no clothes on and was in the hospital garb. When you're in intensive care, the nurses really take care of you extremely well, thank God for the NHS. One of the nurses spoke to me and said, 'You all looked in a really bad way last night when they brought you in. Smoke inhalation can kill you before the fire.'

I was coughing a lot by then, black mucus was coming out, and I had a massive headache for days. It felt like I had been sucking on exhaust fumes, for days afterward. After two days I really needed the toilet and the nurse said she would show me where. I followed her. I was a bit zombified, and I saw Frank sit up in his bed and I said, 'One flew over the cuckoo's nest', and he laughed. Then I asked one of the nurses where Jelone was, and they said he was in a private room and still under sedation; he had been out for three days. I started to think 'Please don't let him die.' I wasn't sure about anything.

Frank came over to my bed and I asked him why the police were there. He didn't know but said he would find out. I had no phone with me, so I couldn't let anybody know; probably just as well, they would only worry. I had no family in London. Lying in the hospital you feel helpless and time goes by really slowly, but we were in good hands.

Frank's mum came to see him, and he could wear his clothes; they were going to let him out. Great news. He told me the police were there to check nobody died. Jelone was stable but still under sedation because of his asthma, they had to be careful. Frank left later that afternoon after three days.

The hospital was doing more tests on me because of my heart problems. I really wanted to get out. I had no idea what state my flat was in, and whether I would be able to move back in or not.

Julian, my mate from Manchester, turned up to visit me. He made me laugh and cheered me up. My wallet was back in the flat, so he gave me £50; I would need it. The next day the doctors told me I could leave. I gathered my things and thanked the nurses, went and saw Jelone, who was still under sedation, and then I left. I had no keys to get into the flat. I rang Notting Hill Housing, and they told me to wait outside my flat and somebody would meet me. The Housing Officer came, and we entered the flat. The place had been an inferno, everything had been burnt, all I had was the clothes I stood in. I had no insurance, but I was still alive.

My flat was not liveable. They placed me in emergency accommodation in a hotel in Fulham. I gathered my thoughts. Over the next few days, I was talking with Notting Hill Housing; they were trying to find me a temporary flat.

After about eight days Jelone was brought out of sedation. I went straight around to the hospital. Jelone's mother had flown over from Los Angeles and had been by his bedside for days, worried sick. She was over the moon when he came around. I explained everything to her, and I spoke with Jelone; he was still groggy and had burns on his arms, but he was going to survive, thank God. The irony; the night before the fire he was at a fundraiser for the firemen.

Eventually, Notting Hill Housing found me a place to live near Holland Park. I was very thankful. It had nothing in there, but I didn't care, how lucky was I?

Things were looking up. Phil and Di gave me bedding and towels. Dave Renegade, a DJ and musician, gave me some clothes, and people offered me money: an old school friend, Paul Weaver, and Ian Piers Dakin from Warrington whose son Jack had been killed, the drummer in the young band Viola Beach, from my hometown of Warrington; I refused but thanked them for their kindness. Gradually I started to get my life back in order. I got a fridge, furniture and my new place came together. I thanked my lucky stars: Frank was safe, Jelone recovered, and his mother decided he should return to Los Angeles as the sun would help with his recovery.

Dear Bad Luck Let's Break Up

Shepherd's Bush is a district of west London, England, within the London Borough of Hammersmith and Fulham 4.9 miles (7.9 km) west of Charing Cross, and identified as a major metropolitan centre in the London Plan.

Although primarily residential in character, its focus is the shopping area of Shepherd's Bush Green, with the Westfield London shopping centre a short distance to the north. The main thoroughfares are Uxbridge Road, Goldhawk Road, and Askew Road, all with small and mostly independent shops, pubs, and restaurants. The Loftus Road football stadium in Shepherd's Bush is home to Queens Park Rangers.

I started to settle into the new flat in 2018. I wondered how the next 12 months would pan out for me. I liked living near Shepherd's Bush, as it was teeming with life, and right on my doorstep was Holland Park, one of the most exclusive parts of London. I was living beside some of the wealthiest in society, including Simon Cowell. I hated *The X-Factor*. I would also see footballer David Beckham, who I would often spot on the streets of High St Kensington.

Just behind me was the largest urban indoor shopping centre in Europe, Westfields, full of designer shops, and people spending ridiculous amounts of money. I much preferred the Old Shepherd's Bush Market, which was run by Muslims selling their wares to all and sundry. I loved walking through there; it was vibrant and interesting, full of colour and cheap tack. I was still carrying on with the Monday Nights at Mau Mau; it wasn't easy, but I persevered, and it was somewhere to go for the local musicians to play and hone their skills. It was still free entry, but the beers had gone up from £2.50 to £4; it was never easy getting people there. Some Mondays were buzzing and others it was quiet. I still enjoyed myself, and felt I was doing my bit for the community.

I was still managing Pink Cigar, who I drove to Paris in my old Renault; I squeezed everybody in and hit the road, taking the ferry across, and arriving in Paris just in time for the gig. They played to a packed house of rock 'n' rollers who loved them. I fell in love with Paris. I could see myself living there if the opportunity ever arises. That night I slept in the car and the band carried on partying through the night. A Pink Cigar party involved lots of beer, and great looking women. I awoke the next day stiff all over, freezing. I collected the band and drove back to London with the boys in high spirits. The glamour of it soon wore off we could barely breathe it was so rammed in the tiny Renault. I carried on through the night, finally dropping them all off at their respective homes dotted around London, and collapsing on my own bed when I finally arrived home exhausted.

I had great neighbours in my area. Patrizia, the Italian girl, was a brilliant photographer who had lived in London for 10 years. I would often say hello when we met on the way out. I would see her at various gigs clicking away with her camera. Across the road from me was Robert Jones, the lead guitarist in the Electrics. Robert was the cousin of David Bowie and a good man who I would often stop and chat with. Phoenix the Egyptian, who had taken loads of photos of ska bands over the years, lived around the corner, so it wasn't long before I felt at home in the area.

I was going backwards and forwards every 2 weeks collecting my son Tommy Jr and bringing him back to London. We would go to the Cuban Boxing Academy, run by Marcus from Cuba and Londoner Mica. It was a great club and only a 5-minute walk from where I lived. Tommy was training twice a week also at Titchfield Boxing Academy near where he lived. He was doing well at school and was very sporty. In the school holidays, we would go to St Ives in Cornwall and stay in a tent in our friends' backyard. Nick and Rebecca would have the tent all ready for our arrival. They would take us fishing and we always had a great time thanks to their hospitality. I have so many happy memories of this little Cornish village, it truly is a magical place and well worth the 6-hour train journey from London's Paddington to get there and have a break from city life. Time was whizzing by so quickly; I couldn't believe it had all gone in the blink of an eye.

There were a lot of council estates around me and I would spot all the young dealers flying by on their BMXs making their deliveries for their punters. There was a spate of stabbings in the area; it was always the youngsters fighting for their turf. As

Madonna once said about London, it didn't matter where you lived, you were always within spitting distance of a council estate. There were monthly silent marches for the victims of the Grenfell disaster. I could see the burnt-out block of flats, which had now been covered up, from my balcony. It was a tragedy that should never have happened in the Borough of Kensington and Chelsea. Every time I passed by the block of flats it was a stark reminder of the people who had lost their lives so tragically. What seemed to be a simple cost-cutting exercise had brought such devastating results to the residents of North Kensington, it truly was a crying shame.

The contract I had signed with Pink Cigar had run out and they found a new manager. To be honest, I was glad for them. I had been there at their first gig 8 years before, in 2009, and now they deserved fresh impetus. The music business was ruthless and the hardest game in the world and I truly hoped good things would happen for them. I never had the money to carry them any further, being realistic. I had been working with musicians for nigh on twenty years and they were predominantly the only people I hung with. Notting Hill was so full of characters, and the market on Portobello Road drew people from all over the world, you never knew who you would bump into from one day to the next, rich man, poor man, musicians, actors, all made their way down Portobello Road at some point. Life moved on, people came and went to Notting Hill and the surrounding areas.

Steve Dior was going backwards and forwards to Mexico. Both his parents had died and left a small fortune from their estate, a hotel and a block of flats; rumour had it that he had given a lot to charity. Good luck to him. His son, Jez Dior, who lives in Los Angeles, had been signed to Epic records and was making a name for himself in the hip hop world. I liked Steve, he had weaned himself off heroin and would come and play at the Mau Mau when he was in town. We had fun. I kept telling Steve to write a book. He had history stretching back to 1975 and the punk scene. He had been close to Sid Vicious, and had played with various members of the New York Dolls when he had been living in the States.

Another great friend of mine was Alan Clayton from the Dirty Strangers, a great rock and roll band from Shepherd's Bush.

I did a bit of casual work with Alan on a job he was running for Bernie Eccleston's accountant, scraping paint off the walls. Al could see my heart wasn't in it and we stuck to doing gigs. I avoided the building sites from then on. Al had worked all over the world with the Stones, but he was just as happy fronting the Dirty Strangers.

Music is such a powerful outlet; it brought me close to many creative people and it made me feel alive. I will always be grateful for that. I had truly immersed myself in the underground music of London, working with all kinds of musicians who came from all over the planet - South Korea to Brazil, Australia, America, all over Europe and beyond - to play on a Monday night at Mau Mau. Money was tight, but what the hell, I was still alive.

I decided to start writing my autobiography. I took a quarter ounce of sniff and started to write the story. I hardly slept for 11 days and wrote continually through the night. I was exhausted but the bare bones of a story appeared. I wrote it all by hand in diaries. I was writing like a maniac, dredging up childhood memories of sexual abuse; in a way it was cathartic. It made me realise I had been carrying these demons around in my head for over 40 years. I had told nobody. Perhaps it was time to get rid of my demons and talk about who had abused me. I booked myself in for 12 sessions. It wasn't easy. I went to the Bard, close by to where I was living. They were also dealing with victims of the Grenfell disaster at the same time.

Over a three month period I unburdened myself and let it all out. It was awfully hard at first; it was highly emotional; the shrink would listen patiently and just pass me a few tissues. It helped me. It was almost like I cried for a childhood that I lost and which was destroyed through no fault of my own, which was true. I had completed the sessions, and I felt better able to deal with the thoughts that had haunted me over all these years; finally, I had done something about them. It was now time to put the memories to bed and move on in my life, which I felt I could now. I had finally confronted my demons.

I went back to the book and started to look for an editor who could make sense of my writing. First, I had to raise money, so my good friend Allison suggested I set up a fundraiser on

Facebook, which I did. Over the months friends and family donated from around Notting Hill and indeed the world.

Another friend, Key Mcloud, said she knew someone who wrote for the *Guardian* and other newspapers. His name was Thomas Rees, and he lived locally. He was in his late 60s, and he reminded me of the actor John Hurt; I had liked him. He had edited my friend's book. So, my mind was made up. Thomas took the manuscript and over a 6-month period he suggested many changes. I paid him, and felt it was money well spent. I had written the book by hand in five diaries and now I had to find somebody to type it all up. I now realise the first draft of any book must be written and rewritten many times over. It was a long painstaking process; I was learning, if nothing else.

I was wondering if all the effort was worth it; would I find a publisher? Would anybody want to read it? All these thoughts came to my head. I persevered. An old friend from Warrington, Janice Stretton, said she would proofread it, doing a great job. I still thought the book needed more work. Another old friend who I had not seen from Warrington, since I was 14, contacted me, Anna Carrington; she was a teacher and we had gone to the same school, Beamont Technical. She suggested more changes to make it more cohesive, so once again I was rewriting the book, trying to make it better. It was keeping my mind occupied, on the job in hand. It was frustrating at times, but I knew I had to see it through till the end with grim determination one way or the other.

'Remember people are only guests in your story, the same way you are only a guest in theirs, so make the story worth reading'
- Lauren Klarfield

In 2018, I was introduced to Mandy De'Ath by my mate Phoenix, the photographer. Mandy was a physiotherapist and had been in the army. Very spiritual, she shared the same birthday as my father, 13th of March, which I took as a good sign.

Mandy was so easy to chat with and we got along. Soon she was to become a good mate of mine who I could trust. At the time I met Mandy I had just started writing my first book.

She had a story to tell herself, and what she told me shocked me to the core, about her fortunate escape from a psychopath, who was still at large conning and abusing vulnerable women, the elderly, and even children.

He pretends to be a Cuban called Santito/Santos Felipe; he is a con artist with multiple dangerous personalities who was known as Flash on the 80s/90s London hip hop scene. Evidence and allegations relating to this man have been given to the police which they have failed to investigate appropriately!

She told me she met him back in summer 2015 at a swing/jazz dance festival in Greenwich, where she was born. She started seeing this person, who called himself Santos, over the summer period, without realising that he was coercing and controlling her, as narcissistic psychopaths do, gaining access to her bank account, smashing her phone, hacking her social media accounts, including closing her Facebook account so she lost all contact with family and friends. She had come from a tough working-class background and went to school in Eltham, South East London, a district within the Royal Borough of Greenwich. She had grafted as a kid to get to where she was today, and against all the odds she had always stood up for herself; yet, she said, she had let this guy abuse her in every way possible, including physical, mental, financial and sexual abuse. She felt lucky to be alive to tell her story, as all of his previous victims have either disappeared mysteriously or committed suicide. She had also found that he has links to the notorious Dolphin Square SW1V address which is where Jimmy Saville and lots of other big-time paedophile rings had operated from.

He was a typical cold non-empathetic psychopath, who displayed superficial charm and went to the extremes of conning his victims into believing he was a Cuban by learning to speak fluent Spanish and Italian. He fooled his victims and got them to believe he was a religious pastor who built churches for third world countries. He took money from them by pretending it would help build his fake churches.

149

Fortunately, her line manager knew of her story of abuse; he had also been a victim of Santos. She had managed to get away from him, but he had somehow found out where she was working in Windsor, and called up her workplace, screaming and shouting down the phone abuse to her work colleagues, demanding to know where she was and pretending to be her boss. Her line manager, fortunately, had been incredibly supportive of her.

He was still stalking and harassing her by turning up to where she was living and working, just to put the fear into her to let her know he was still around. She said that this was a big case and if it was investigated properly there would be some big names who would be highlighted with some extraordinary findings.

I really couldn't fathom how she was going to sort it out. She is on the case now as I write this and corresponding with journalists.

We arranged to meet again, and she convinced me to come along to the Spiritual Church in Notting Hill, the following week. Mandy goes regularly to spiritual churches all over London. When the time came, I went along with an open mind, deep down believing it was all mumbo jumbo though.

Notting Hill Spiritual Church

This church was built in the early years of the twentieth century. The land was purchased by the Beard family following spirit direction which guided them to stables belonging to William Whitley's Store. A trust was formed, and the church was erected on this site, and consecrated in October 1912. Contrary to what many may believe, spiritualist meetings are not held in darkened rooms where one 'calls up the dead.' Our friends and loved ones who have passed from this phase of life still wish to communicate with us, just as they would if they had moved to another part of the world. Through the gift of mediumship continuance of life after death can be proven.

Spiritual healing is freely given and can assist in conventional treatment given by the medical profession. Often it can also alleviate illness which fails to respond to other forms of treatment.

We sat down in the church and the medium started talking. There were about 50 people in the congregation. The medium spoke to various people during the course of the service, and then he pointed at me. I was quite shocked. He said, 'I have two people here who want to talk with you.'

'Who?' I replied, thinking this was a load of bollocks.

He said, 'Their names Robert and Dave, and they are quite insistent to speak with you.' My jaw fell: of all the random names in the world he could pick he chose them two names, Rob my lifelong friend who had died of pleurisy 8 years before and my uncle Dave who had died of prostate cancer in 2013. I had never met this medium in my life, this was my first time coming to a spiritual church.

I really was shellshocked. He said, 'I have them both here and they are talking over each other.' He explained my uncle Dave said he wanted to say goodbye to his family, and for them not to worry. He had been really embarrassed with his illness in the last few months of his life, and had not wanted to see people because of it, Dave was a man's man. I could understand where he was coming from; he told me to get out of London, to look for a garden and a pathway, I wasn't sure what he meant; years before, my friend Rike had said the same when I was in Thailand.

Then Rob spoke. He had been cruelly taken away unexpectedly at the age of 49, and he was still angry about it. He missed his family, his mum and dad and his two beautiful daughters, but he was watching over them. I just couldn't take it all in. It felt so surreal. After the service was over, we left the church and I was just numb. I couldn't believe what had just transpired. Mandy, who goes regularly to spiritual churches all over London, said she wasn't surprised at all; she said every time she goes and takes people for the first time the medium speaks to them. I just kept thinking I cannot believe what has just happened. I had always thought it was just nonsense. I swear to God I really was stunned beyond words. I walked Mandy to the tube station, and she went home, and I spent all night thinking about what had happened.

Rob Taylor had two daughters. Chloe, who went on to study at Goldsmiths College, fell into a great job. Rubi is a singer who is just about to release a track 'The Invisible People' in the style of soul/NuJazz; she has a great voice, reminds me of Lily Allen and Amy Whitehouse combined. Rob would be so enormously proud of both of them. Their mother Theresa got remarried to Simon Williams and lives close by to me. I am sure Rob is looking down on all of them with a massive smile on his face, when he sees how life is panning out for them all.

A week later I took Tommy up to Warrington, and we stayed with my mate Claire, and her daughters Cydney and Georgia. I was out walking the dog a few days later with Claire, behind her house, and we came through a pathway of green, and I stopped dead in my tracks. This was it. We were standing where the medium said I would be. I think they had been telling me about this walkway to let me know that it had actually happened, and their spirits were real; it was the only explanation I could think of at the time, but I am now a firm believer that some spirits are out there, especially the ones who felt cheated in death.

There are things far beyond my comprehension; I now firmly believe that spirits are out there. People may think I'm crazy. The spiritual meeting has convinced me I'm not. After the break, I dropped Tommy home and came back to London.

West End Girls and East End Boys

I gave up the car as it was becoming a liability, and started to go to gigs by public transport. Squeezing into the rush hour crowds on the Central Line was no joke in the summer heat, especially when there was no air conditioning - trying not to touch anybody, clinging on to the upright poles, you could smell the sweat of some of the passengers and you were in such close proximity it could be embarrassing. The tube seemed to take ages getting to Oxford Circus. You could sense the irritation of the other passengers when you had to make your move to pass through the doors of the tube, to get onto the platform, at your destination.

It made me wonder why I had stayed so long in London. The years just seemed to pass by so quickly all in a blur really. One year seemed to blend into the next, with no real sense of time or reality. Sometimes I would wonder which year it was. Most people I knew lived in small flats with no gardens, rents were awfully expensive, and people lived in sheds at friends' houses, or spent years living on couches or sofa surfing.

This city attracted everybody. It was exciting and everything was here, but there was a price to be paid. The constant traffic fumes, the traffic jams, the relentlessness of it all could drive you crazy at times.

I made my way up the escalators, heading to the 100 Club. I had to get rid of my car as it was becoming far too expensive: parking, petrol, tax, and insurance. In reality I never needed a car, there was so much public transport to choose from in this city of lost souls. If you were loaded, to a certain degree isolated from it all, living in large houses, travelling by black cabs as most of the rich did, they never really mixed with the normal people.

Maybe it was good for Tommy to be growing up near the sea now - I missed him like crazy but he was safe and happy, that was the main thing.

I arrived at the 100 Club just in time for the sound check. I had come to watch my mates, The Electrics, who were playing that evening. Alan Blizzard the front man was a good friend who had done me many favours. I asked him if he wanted a drink. He looked at me and laughed, saying are you feeling ok? I laughed back and went to the bar and got him one. That's the last one till Xmas now Al, I said as I passed it to him. The live music scene is not as vibrant as it was 30 years ago in London. Going to the gigs was always fun, you would know loads of people and you felt at home when you knew the band and their crowds. The Electrics had a great crowd, mainly people who are in their 50s, who still had that deep passion for music from being teenagers in the punk days.

Dale Senior was a taxi driver a mate of Alan's. He also sang and played with the Kult 45s, a huge bear of a man with a mad sense of humour; it was always good to catch up with them. After the gig, I hung around for a while then made my way up the stairs and caught the night bus home.

I missed traveling the world so much. I was seeing posts from friends on Facebook in far-flung places, Peru, Ecuador, Cambodia, Columbia, a continual reminder that there is life going on outside of London.

People were leaving London; some were forced out by expensive rents. London still had a hold on me: everything was here on your doorstep. Some people still tried to get me involved in scams and drug deals, but I knew where that life would lead me, easy money, and at some point, a prison cell; I wasn't prepared to go back to that life anymore.

I most certainly didn't want that life for my son, so I carried on with the music. I didn't have to worry about the police knocking on my door. I had tried many things over the years, extra work in films and TV, working the markets, running people around by car, doing odd jobs, anything to survive. I deeply appreciated being alive.

My brother Anthony had now been living in Dubai for twelve years. Six of them had been on the run from the authorities over there. They had his passport and he couldn't leave because his business partner had borrowed a lot of money, and fled Dubai leaving our kid in the shit and with no way of repaying the money.

He had been jailed twice for 6 months, and they let him out to repay the loans; he was like an indentured slave, having his own nightmare there. He had a Philippine girlfriend and they shared a tiny room with five others, but much like me he was a survivor. If he couldn't sort this out, he would have to go to prison for a further 3 years.

I felt helpless, unable to help him. I just hoped his luck would turn for the better. My sister Lynn must have shaken her head at times, the scrapes both of her brothers got into; we just had to carry on and hope for the best.

In February of 2019 Slydigs released this statement on their Facebook page:

Slydigs, from Burtonwood, have said in a joint statement that they are going to take a break to freshen things up and pursue individual projects. But they are leaving fans with a parting gift as the four-piece have also announced they will be releasing an EP of songs recorded with producer Brendan Lynch, who has worked with Paul Weller, Primal Scream and Ocean Colour Scene.

Former Warrington Music Festival headliners Slydigs are certainly leaving on a high as the rock and roll band were handpicked to tour America and Europe with The Who for their 50th-anniversary celebrations.

In a statement to fans, Slydigs said: 'As artists, we believe that there has to be a constant flow of change and without that life can sometimes become stale. We set out on this journey to reach as high as we possibly could, and we achieved so much. We were proud to be the underdogs and our mission statement from the outset was, of course, never to be tamed. While we know that this news will be saddening for a lot of you, we still believe we have a lot more to give.

'We will be boarding our own, individual ships to head for new horizons and hope to meet up again someday. We are all still very much brothers and wish each other the best of luck in our alternative routes.

'We would like to thank Trinifold Management for all the help and efforts in giving us the opportunity to travel around the world playing in front of thousands of you that have become long-standing fans.

'Also, a huge shout out to Adrian Burns, International Talent Booking, X-ray Touring, and Tommy Kennedy IV, for their much-valued efforts and endeavours. We cannot thank enough, most importantly, the fans we have picked up along the way. Without you, we wouldn't have had the experiences of a lifetime that we have had so far.'

It made me sad when I heard this. Dean has started a new band, Standin Man, with drummer Pete Fleming. I wish them all the best in all of their future endeavours.

'Success is going from failure to failure with no loss of enthusiasm'
                                        - Winston Churchill

Chapter Eight

Smiley and the Underclass were progressing, making a name outside of London; they had just returned from a tour of Japan and Europe. I loved their song 'It's All England'. They were a true representation of multicultural London. Vince Powers from the Mean Fiddler had reopened the Subterania under the Westway and brought in big names like Van Morrison, Jimmy Cliff, and Killing Joke, to name a few, to satisfy the music lovers in Notting Hill and beyond.

I would run into Tom Vague, who wrote about the history of the Notting Hill music scene, its past musical history, and Ishmael Blagrove, a writer and filmmaker who is currently writing a book on the history of the frontline of Notting Hill and Ladbroke Grove. I have seen excerpts and it looks good; a highly intelligent man, with a passion for defending injustices. Aidan MacManus is a historian and DJ who works for Portobello Radio, a cheeky chappy from Harlesden; the place is full of character, which I love about West London. With his producer Greg Weir, they do great shows for the community.

I was backwards and forwards to the Mau Mau, meeting bands and chatting about upcoming gigs. It was a passion to keep the scene alive, rather than a money-making thing; I figured it was good for my karma if nothing else.

I would occasionally pop into the Ripe Tomato, a high-end pizza restaurant on the All Saints Road. It was run by David Coley and his family for 25 years. David was a gregarious guy, along with his wife Ethel, who had been in the groundbreaking musical show *Hair*, and they had two children, Daniel and Alexia, who was a great singer who performed with the Rotten Hill Gang, along with Hollie Cook, the daughter of the legendary drummer from the Sex Pistols, Paul Cook. Whenever the Rotten Hill Gang played, you never knew who would turn up and play; they were an ensemble of four to ten or twelve band members at times, it was always a good night.

Notting Hill was vibrant but losing some of its characters due to the exceedingly high rents and the gentrifying of the area. If you looked hard enough, you could still find the real Notting Hill. The Tabernacle in Powis Square served the west Indian community, and there were great gigs there also. The Globe had been there since 1959 and had been run by Keith for years, until he sold up. It was a small place but a great place to meet locals, and it's still there.

There's the local Portobello Radio, run by Piers Thompson, and Chris Sullivan, interviewing locals and keeping the community informed of what's happening in the area; there is more to Notting Hill than meets the eye for the casual visitor, if they know where to look.

2018 came and went and we entered into 2019. I was reconnecting with old friends via Facebook from Warrington, like Johnny Woods, who I had worked with in London 35 years before, in my bricklaying days. A larger than life character, who loved a joke - Warrington is full of them. Facebook can suck up your time, but it also has its good points. I had spent Xmas with Allison, and her family, and Frank from Mau Mau came over; he was just back from France. My son Tommy came, and we had a good day. A few days later Frank flew out to Mexico to join up with Steve Dior.

Frank had been a good friend to me. Sandra was also a good friend. People were moving on with their lives and it was time for me to make some positive changes. I quit smoking, carried on working on my book and looked to the future with optimism. January is always a bleak month. I got on with the Mondays at Mau Mau, now in its fifth year. My mate Alan from the Dirty Strangers had sold his house in Shepherd's Bush and moved out with his wife Jacquie to Chichester. Their son Paul stayed in London and was running a monthly rock night at the Troubadour in Earls Court, which was always a good night, and it was a good chance to catch up with Big Al, as he was affectionately known.

I was sending the manuscript back and forth making changes, tweaking it, rewriting bits, and I was wondering if I would ever get it finished.

Pink Cigar were playing all over London; I went sometimes but felt a bit awkward with their new manager on the scene. I would usually leave on their last song. I would have a drink with Sid the drummer occasionally; he lived near me. I had known him since he was 16, time was passing by so quickly. Portobello Live Festival came around again. Micky P had all the venues in the area covered. It brought life to the area. We all had a good time over the May Bank Holiday. It was two days of live music in glorious weather.

When the school holidays started in the summer, I collected Tommy, and we had our annual trip to St Ives, camping in the backyard of Nick's gaff. I was truly happy; the weather was brilliant. After the holidays were over Tommy returned home. I always missed him, but if he was happy, so was I.

Having finally finished the book I sent it off to three publishers and they expressed an interest and I decided to go with New Haven Publishing. A contract was sent to me. I arranged to meet Teddie Dahlin, who ran the company; she was based in Norway. We arranged to meet at the Hilton Hotel on Edgware Road. We met, had a drink, and parted ways. She sent it off to Sarah, one of her editors, and over the next few months a date was set to release the book on the 22nd of August 2019. I had done my bit, now it was in the hands of the publisher. My mate Alan Blizzard is a graphic designer and he did a great cover for the book. It was sent over to New Haven and they did the rest.

Wembley

My friend from Qatar, who I had gone to school with, sent a message he would be coming to London for four days. Warrington were in the Challenge Cup Final at Wembley. He had bought tickets; it was always good to see him. It was the weekend of Notting Hill Carnival. I knew it would be a massive weekend of boozing.

The weeks and months sped by and finally Paul arrived. He booked himself into the Dorset hotel, next to Shepherd's Bush Empire. I went and met him later that night, and we went to the 100 Club on Oxford Street to watch Brian James from the Damned, along with the Electrics, and big Alan Clayton was on the bill. It was a top night and we headed home in the early hours by cab, waking up the next day feeling a bit rough. My book had been released the day before, titled *Nightmare in Jamaica*.

We took the train to Wembley. It was a really hot day. We met up with friends Richard from Camden and Sweeney, an old school friend who now lived in Bath. We had a good few drinks in some Brazilian bar before the game. When we headed to the game I was feeling a bit weird. Warrington beat St Helens and the crowd went wild.

Afterward, we went to a restaurant in Marylebone. I bade them all farewell and headed home totally wasted and crashed out. The first day of the Carnival was the next day, and I wandered around and bumped into Patricia, the Portuguese lady who had taken some great photos of Tommy Jr over the years. She was with her boyfriend Michael from Belgium. We shook hands. I still felt a bit rough and decided to go home and lie down, hoping to feel better the next day.

I woke up early on the main day of the Carnival. It was Bank Holiday Monday, and over a million people turned up including my mate from Birmingham, Mick, and Paul, with Richard, turned up. We had a ball, drinking and partying, and finished off later that night in the Mau Mau Bar. Eventually after a long day and night we all went our separate ways.

I stayed home the next day, and at around six in the evening, I went food shopping, came home, and could barely make it up the stairs. I was feeling strange. My phone rang while I was lying on the couch; it was my friend Jay. I told him how I was feeling and he jumped in his car and came over to see me. He rang the bell. I staggered over and pressed the intercom button and let him in. He looked at me and said Tommy you are not well I'm going to ring an ambulance. I was too fucked to disagree. Twenty minutes later two paramedics came up the stairs and checked me over and decided to take me to the nearest hospital, Charing Cross in Hammersmith. I felt like shit. I was transferred later that night to the hospital on Ducane Road.

The doctors looked me over and told me I'd had a heart attack; they would perform an operation immediately on me. They performed keyhole surgery. A couple of hours later, they informed me the operation was unsuccessful, my arteries were so damaged they had decided I would need a further operation in a few days' time, it would be a triple bypass.

I asked the doctor what this would involve. He explained your arteries get narrowed when fatty deposits build up on the inner walls of your arteries. The aim of coronary bypass surgery is to bypass - or 'get around' - the narrowed sections of your coronary arteries. The surgeon does this by grafting a blood vessel between the aorta (the main blood vessel leaving the heart) and a point along the coronary artery, past the narrowed area.

In most cases, at least one of the blood vessels used as a bypass graft is an artery from your chest called the internal mammary artery. Blood vessels such as a vein from your legs and sometimes an artery from your arms are used for the other grafts. You can have one graft, but it's more common to have two, three, or four (often called double, triple, or quadruple bypasses).

If your surgeon needs to cut your breastbone, you will have a long wound down the middle of your chest. If you have had a vein graft from your leg or an artery graft from your arm, you will have a smaller wound in these places too.

A heart-lung bypass machine circulates the blood around your body while the surgeon operates on your heart, but some surgeons carry out coronary bypass operations without this machine. This is called beating heart surgery.

What happens after surgery?

After your operation you will be moved to intensive care for close monitoring until you wake up. Once your condition is stable, you will be moved to the high dependency unit or the cardiac ward.

I lay back and thought fuck, just my luck. Thank God for the NHS once again. I thanked them and rang Jay, to thank him for his quick thinking; he had most certainly saved my life that night.

So once again I had been lucky in my unluckiness: I would have surely been dead without his help. I'd had so many near-death experiences I felt there must be somebody watching over me from somewhere.

The summer heat in the hospital was stifling. I was googling about the operation on my phone. Hanging around waiting for the operation was dragging. Some friends came and saw me in the hospital: Al from the Dirty Strangers, Ewa the polish girl, Sharon from Fulham, Lucinda who worked on the stalls selling vintage clothes. My Japanese friend Jay brought me things I needed; to be honest I didn't really want people to see me in this state. I was worried about my son Tommy. I wondered if I would be around for his 12th birthday in April. All kinds of things go through your mind while you are waiting for a major operation.

I didn't tell my daughter Sophie. I couldn't see what the point was - she had enough on her plate bringing three kids up. I made friends with the other patients, cracking jokes to lift our spirits. People sent me books and magazines to keep my mind occupied. Finally the day of the operation came around. They shaved my chest and legs and wheeled me into the operating theatre and I gave a silent prayer that I would survive. They filled me full of drugs and I was gone in an instant, knocked out completely.

The operation took 3 or 4 hours. They had cut my leg open and removed the good vein, opened my breastbone, and rewired the blockages in my heart. I felt like I woke up in the middle of it all. I shit myself but I was more than likely hallucinating.

When they did bring me around, I was in intensive care with a tube down my throat and unable to talk, gagging slightly, covered in sweat, disorientated. The main thing was I was still alive, thank fuck. I thought of family. I had a mild infection in my chest wound and a frozen shoulder, and the doctors told me I may have to be operated on again; oh no, the thought of going through it all again was freaking me out over the next few days. I was so full of drugs I felt like I was on acid, tripping, and was in the middle of a rave; really weird emotions kept coming and going while I lay there waiting to be operated on again. By some good fortune the infection went away and they decided there was no need to operate again, thank God.

I was kept in the ICU for a further 5 days, before they trundled me back to a ward to recover. I was being fed Oxycodone opiate-based for the pain, I felt like I was on smack; it wasn't such a bad feeling and it kept the pain at bay.

I was struggling to walk when after 3 weeks they decided to discharge me. Man, was I happy. I staggered out of the hospital and hailed a cab, arriving home 20 minutes later.

Count Your Blessings Not Your Troubles

I realised it was going to be difficult looking after myself. Luckily, my sister came down to London and took care of me for a few days. Her husband Pete drove down and drove us all back to their house on the south coast. I stayed up in their spare room for 4 weeks, while I regained my strength. My sister nursed me back to health just like she had done 20 years ago for my father who had the same operation.

The time came for me to return to London and look after myself. My brother-in-law ran me back.

Over the next few weeks, I weaned myself off the Oxycodone, and I started to heal, going on long walks and eating healthily. My good friend Wiggsy the musician from Taurus Trakker had been running Mau Mau Mondays in my absence and did a grand job. Some friends started to move out of London; Steve Dior moved back to Mexico, another good friend Billy Idle moved to Ibiza, and Frank moved out to Devon; good luck to them.

With all that had gone on, I had not had a book launch, so I spoke with Teddie at New Haven Publishing and they sent me a couple of boxes of books. I fixed the date at the Mau Mau, Saturday 14th of December, and decided to launch the book. I had bands playing, The Electrics and a Jamaican band called Etchoo based in Harlesden. A good friend OJ Jennings was also to play.

The night of the launch came. The Mau Mau was rammed out with friends who bought copies. I sold all the books apart from 6 copies. It was a top night. A few days later I gave a reading at the

Troubadour for the Dirty Strangers Xmas Party for my mate Al, and his son Paul; it was loads of fun. I sold the remaining 6 copies.

It was almost Xmas and on Xmas Eve I went to my sister's again on the coast. A few days after New Year 2020 I returned to London.

I was feeling fighting fit and ready for anything. I did a podcast with Shaun Attwood, the writer who had given me a quote for my book along with writer Mandasue Heller, from my hometown of Warrington. Chris Salewicz also gave me a quote.

My book, *Nightmare in Jamaica*, had been mentioned in the *Guardian*. I decided to finish the sequel, *Notting Hill Ponces*. I signed up to do a creative writing course. Life is truly an adventure full of twists and turns; whatever happens, embrace it all.

Finally, I got some good news from my brother Anthony, who had been living in Dubai for the last 12 years by now. He had been well and truly stitched up by one of his business partners, who had borrowed a shed load of money from the banks in Dubai, then had fucked off back to Ireland, saying he would be back in a few weeks' time. He never returned, leaving our kid to be the fall guy. He has been living his own nightmare in Dubai, these last six years. Living illegally, unable to pay the £100,000 back; they jailed him twice under horrendous conditions. Ultimately, he'd had enough, and he was prepared to go back to jail for a further 3 years to get the case off his back. He went from living the high life to sharing a small room with six Philippines with no money to his name, unable to drive and in a very bad situation indeed through no fault of his own.

A couple of friends rallied around after all the shit he had been through and lent him something like £10,000, and he made the offer to the subcontractor saying 'Take this money or I will go back to jail for 3 years. You will end up with nothing.' Luckily calling his bluff worked, and the offer was accepted, the best Xmas present our kid ever got. He is allowed to travel outside of Dubai, and get his driving licence back, and is now working legally and planning to retire to the Philippines in the next 5 or 10 years. He had been put through so much stress his hair had gone grey virtually overnight, but fair play to him, he battled on to get this final result and we all breathed a huge sigh of relief for him.

The start of 2020 was looking promising at long last; surely it was going to be much better than the last few years. I carried on with Mau Mau Mondays. I knew the bar was up for sale, but so far, nobody had made an offer. It was a slow start to the year but gradually people started to get over the Xmas blues, and came out to party again towards the end of January, one of the most depressing months of the year. We entered February. The news had been full of a virus coming out of China called the coronavirus, but we were not taking that much notice of it in the UK at the time.

Phil, the Irishman who used to help me run the bands around, and did me a lot of favours in his car, sadly died in January 2020. Ginty organised the funeral. His family and friends saw him off at Kensal Rise Crematorium, and we all went back to the Pig and Whistle in North Kensington, and had a few drinks in his honour. North Kensington is an area of west London, north of Notting Hill and south of Kensal Green and in the Royal Borough of Kensington and Chelsea. The names North Kensington and Ladbroke Grove describe the same area.

North Kensington was once known for its slum housing, but housing prices have now risen and the area, on the whole, is considered exclusive and upmarket, although expensive residences are interspersed with lower-income areas like the Lancaster West Estate.

Jay, and Frank, the owners, had found some buyers who were interested in buying the Mau Mau Bar from them. It looked like the deal was going through. I had been putting gigs on at the Mau Mau for 16 years; wow, where had that time gone? A few weeks later we had the final party, and the next day, the bar was closed. The new owners started the refurbishments. It was due to reopen sometime in the spring of 2020. The end of an era indeed. I'm sure the Mau Mau Bar will go down in Portobello Road history - and I can only say, it was a pleasure to be a small part of it. It was the meeting place for me and many others over the years. I have very happy memories of all the people and bands I met there over the 16 years I worked there.

Several rumours had circulated that the council was behind the closure, or the bar closed due to growing gentrification in the area. Mau Mau Bar owner, Jay Hirano, said he was even asked whether the bar has been sold to Ed Sheeran, who recently opened a pub on Portobello Road. Overall, there has been confusion around the closure and now Jay has revealed the real reason behind it. Jay gave an interview with the local newspaper, *My London News*:

Mr. Hirano said: 'I don't think it's the only council, business rate or rent closing the music venues but people themselves sometimes. In this modern time of 2020, people have other things they want to spend money on, or they have to spend money on rather than £5 door money which goes to musicians.

'As well as business rates, housing rent, and food and all those bills are going up. Closure of music venues is one of the chain reactions of all other problems we have.'

Jay Hirano, who ran Mau Mau Bar for eight years, said owning the venue was one of his biggest life achievements and although it created great memories, it was time for it to end.

A musician himself, Mr. Hirano also contributes to the live music scene as a member of a music band, Smiley and The Underclass, and going forward plans to work on that more.

He said: 'Mau Mau gave me so much, you can't even imagine what I've gained, the number of friends I made and met at the bar is unbelievable and I appreciate everyone who got involved.'

'I had a little bird its name was Enza I opened the window and in flu Enza
 - 1918 Children's Rhyme

Life was ticking on while I was still doing cardio at the hospital; perhaps it was time to take stock of things and reassess my life. It had been many things, but it most certainly had never been boring.

My son Tommy was getting tired of all the travelling backwards and forwards to London on a Friday and back to his home on the coast early Sunday mornings; three years of this. I decided to go and stay there every two weeks. He is 12 now and has his own mind; the time was just whizzing by. I didn't want to miss any of it. We would go to his boxing club on a Friday at Titchfield Boxing Academy and we kept the bond going.

The coronavirus was dominating all the news; thousands had died in China, and Italy was bearing the brunt of it all in Europe at this time.

Eventually, all the borders were being closed and finally in March 2020 the newly elected Prime Minister, Boris Johnson, announced all the pubs and restaurants were to be closed down in this global pandemic and we were all to be locked down. New words were coming into the fray: social distancing, flattening the curve; people were becoming frightened and hysterical. I must admit I had not been taking it too seriously, even though I was in the high-risk category. I was now being forced to take notice.

A few months ago, we were all going along quite merrily and now it felt like the forces of nature were catching up on us with a vengeance. People are being told not to go to work, millions of people around the world are worried they will go bankrupt, they are going to die. I had been through the power cuts of the 70s, the strikes, the Aids epidemic of the 80s, but in my living memory, I had never known anything like this. I've always been an optimist and believe we will come through whatever life throws our way.

My mate the DJ from Warrington, Pete Rigby, rang me and told me to be careful. He was telling me his father had been 19 when the Spanish flu had sprung out of Kansas from a suspected pig farm in 1918; over 50 million people had died worldwide and the death toll in the UK alone had been 228,000. The Spanish flu pandemic had been the deadliest in history; an estimated 500 million people were infected, one-third of the planet at that time.

It made me think history is repeating itself once again. The thing that bothered me the most was I was unable to visit my son Tommy. I was like many unfortunate people in the same position unable to visit family and friends; I would just have to wait until this was over. I rang him daily; if he was happy, so was I, that was the main thing in my eyes.

There were good news stories around the pandemic; people clapped every Thursday night for the NHS frontline staff, who are fighting and battling to save lives, putting their own lives at risk.

The 99-year-old former soldier Captain Tom Moore raised over £33,000,000 for the NHS, by setting up a Just Giving page promising to do a 100 laps of his garden; it had been a family joke he expected to raise £1000, and it went on to be the biggest ever fundraiser on the Just Giving page; people worldwide donated.

These are the facts as they stand now in May 2020.

The first human cases were reported in December 2019. People first began coming down with COVID-19 in the Wuhan region of central China, the World Health Organisation reports. The last time I went out before the pandemic hit the UK was Saturday 8th of March 2020.

My friend Neil, who owns the music shop on the All Saints Road where they repair guitars and sell instruments, had organised a gig at the Italian Job, a pub on the corner of the road. He invited me along to do a reading of *Nightmare in Jamaica* - he had many bands playing also on the night. It was a huge success; all of my friends came along including Allison Trumper and her boyfriend Del from a band called the Satellites, Sandra Clarke, the designer from Wandsworth, Frank, from Devon, Sarah the nurse, Steve Holloway who used to DJ at the Wag Club had lived in Miami for many years, Tony Auguste, a good man, and very intelligent, Alex Shirley the actor, my neighbour Patrizia Tagliatti the photographer, Maz, the French model who lives in London, and Sharon from Fulham who makes hats for festivals. The place was packed. Neil's band the Freak Elite played a blinding set. Little did we realise what was in store. Life is full of twists and turns, but isn't that the beauty of it?

Who knows what is around the corner? I couldn't see myself being happy with the same woman from being 18 and still with her all these years later. Many do, and they are extremely happy; good on them I say.

What is life all about - getting married, settling down, raising children, being a good citizen; at the end of it you still die. You accumulate wealth and work hard - you're still going to die. I think people should just do what makes them happy instead of doing what is expected by society and going along with that. I genuinely believe you must do what makes you happy, whatever that may be. Sure, who wouldn't want to have money, but if you have it does that make you happier? I think it helps you to buy material things and makes your life easier in the financial sense; I still think love is a beautiful thing. If you can meet your soulmate and be happy for the rest of your life - I think you have done well. I will go to my grave no matter what happens believing life is truly an adventure.

Anything that happens or has happened in my life has been an adventure, a joy to be alive; to even feel the pain of sadness makes you realise you are alive. The human spirit is alive in every single one of us, don't take that for granted.

The average life span is 4,700 weeks. When you think that, you truly realise we are just here for a short time. In the big scheme of life, we are only a tiny drop in the humanity of life.

If you can help somebody out for no financial gain and genuinely do something with a clean heart, try it, you will feel much better about yourself.

Thinking back over the years, I had been involved in so many scams and scrapes I was lucky to be still alive. I wondered where I would be in the next five years. I had been taking each day as it came, most of my life, and just living in the moment, no real plans beyond having a good time. Since at the age of 39 I became involved in music, my days have been filled with trying to make other people's dreams come true; some appreciated it, but many didn't.

If you have loads of money in the music business everybody will listen to you and help to relieve you of it at the same time.

It really is a vicious business at the end of the day, but it's the most fun. Would I do it all over again? I would like to think I would.

My son is now 12 years old and I will devote my time to him as much as possible; the family should be everything in this life, above money or material things. It took me many years to finally realise that. I also realise I am a free spirit; being alone is something that I love, as well as something that many find difficult. It's hard to live your life without taking other people's opinions and emotions into account; being a free spirit is making your own decisions and living your life the way you want. Find your lifestyle and buzz off it. It's always good to see my family and friends, especially my son who is not yet fully grown. I want to be around for him till he reaches the age he can look after himself. I am sure he will be very strong-willed and do as he pleases later in life, he is showing signs already and I am glad of that. He should live his life for himself, having his own mind and trusting in his own decisions.

My daughter is also strong-minded. You need this in life. They must be able to think for themselves, and do what makes them happy.

Making your own way in life, being self-aware, and being able to think for yourself are all signs that choosing how things pan out is important to you. Doing things in your own way, and for your own benefit, is something to aim for, not be worried about. Travel; I've been lucky enough to travel, and have loved every second of it. For me, travel is a joy. I know when to be selfish and put myself first; if something turns you on - go for it. It can take years to find that passion that really makes your soul feel good, so when you do find it, go ahead and do it. Find what interests you, and go for it, whatever it is.

Alone time was something that I used to detest.

I've been on my own a few years now, and I live on my own. I still have a life where I go to gigs, but I have also learned to love my own company. If somebody comes along and understands that, who knows what may happen in the future, my mind is always open.

Nobody should ever make you feel like you must sacrifice yourself for them, so make sure you surround yourself with friends, family, and partners who support you.

Being a free spirit doesn't mean abandoning everyone; it means making decisions for yourself and either embracing those who accept that or moving on to things or people that make you feel comfortable. I have friends who I have not seen for years but when we meet it was like yesterday; they know me, I know them, we all have our own lives to live and to lead.

Family and friends are great, but you should never feel trapped and feel compelled to be with them and they should understand and respect that; say no if you must, after all, it's your life. At the end of the day, it's your life and you only get one shot at it, you must do what you feel is right for you and not be a people pleaser. If you feel trapped, do something about it. You hate the job? Quit. You're not happy in a relationship? Leave. Do what makes you feel happy before it's too late.

People who know me well, know I can be quiet and quite guarded, but when I'm 'on one', I absolutely love laughter and messing around. My cousin Darren summed me up once, he said: 'I love our Tommy when he's pissed and on one, but I can't stand him when he's sober.' I do have a serious side and probably I think too much, a bit like a comedian maybe. I've spoken to a few shrinks in my time and I think I would make a good one myself!

I had met guys in the 70s in jail who would walk behind young prisoners, knock them out and drag them in a cell and sodomise them. It never happened to me, but it can teach you to be wary of people. I really could tell a few stories. I once met the child killer Mary Bell - she is out now. The serial killer Peter Sutcliffe, aka the Yorkshire Ripper as he was operating under, ended up in jail around the time I served my last sentence in the UK.

I love people who are easygoing and think differently. A friend of mine said 'You should get into scriptwriting.' I never even thought of things like that, I was too busy trying to survive and fending for myself. I was and am a rolling stone. Finances can dictate your life to a certain degree, but your energy will get you where you are meant to be. I truly believe that.

I spent time around nuns in the 60s; when you're a kid it's quite scary, one minute you're with your mum, and then you're driven there, not having a clue what was going on; me and my sister Lynn, I was only about six. It freaked me out when I realised that was now my new home: no Mummy's kisses, no Daddy's smiles. Welcome to the Convent. Life is so strange; I look and think, what the fuck! They were trying to force-feed me cabbage because you had to clear your plate. I hated it and my sister Lynn would eat it for me. Happy days!

I remember going to the mortuary many years back to see a girl who had died aged 18. If you have not touched a dead body before, they are cold and look waxy. I remember when I was about 15, my uncle Benny died. He was 42 (like my grandfather) and had died of lung cancer. He had been really good-looking and was full of the Glaswegian wit. He had travelled the world and always used to have fun with me. My nana idolised him big time, she was a very loving woman. She nursed him upstairs at her house in the last few months of his life. He didn't want anyone to see him, he was losing his hair. He had been so full of life, but he withered away to nothing. When he died my nana had his body in an open coffin.

My father was talking to him; they were best friends. My dad was telling him how much he loved him and how much he was going to miss him. It was the first time I heard my father cry. My nana took me into the room to see him in the open coffin. I loved my uncle Benny with all my heart, he was a star in our family. He had travelled the world, having grown up in the Gorbals in Glasgow when it was a rough place to be. He had charisma and he had character; I don't care how much money you have, if you don't have charisma and character of some sort, you've got nothing in my eyes.

I was heartbroken. I was going off the rails big time. I looked down at him in the coffin. My nana turned to me and said: 'Did you love him?' I said: 'I did.' She said: 'Don't be scared to touch him then if you loved him in this life, he won't hurt you.' I had been a bit hesitant at first but when she said that it made me touch him and kiss him and say my goodbyes.

Nine months later his sister, my aunty Rita, died. She was 39 and had a brain haemorrhage. Her sister, my mother Margaret (Mother) Mary Theresa Keenan, I really don't know what happened in her life, apart from she came out of a convent in Glasgow and when she was 16 and joined the rest of the family in Warrington. I would like to find out one day, maybe it will help me to understand myself. Nobody really told me anything, it was all kept quiet in those days.

When you look at a disco ball and the lights hit it and the light shoots off in thousands of different directions, that is people's perception of you. We are all different and multi-faceted. When you fall deeply in love and someone loves you back in the same way, love and sex are then a spiritual experience, when you expose your innermost thoughts to each other and don't hold back for fear or favour, you truly become as one, you are deep and meaningful, rather than deep and meaningless. If you have truly been in love with someone you will know what I mean, and it is a beautiful experience.

'Make love not war' is a great saying. We are all driven by our desires and our fears when we are younger, especially when you are still finding yourself. But on the journey we call life, if you find your soulmate, hold on to them whatever your age. We can all be a mass of contradictions and insecurities. We are all products of our environments. If you are still reading this book, I thank you for bearing with me. I've seen things you will never see, and you've seen things that I will never see. But if you meet someone on your wavelength, you can share the same experiences from then on, to a certain degree.

You get to a certain age and you start to learn things about yourself. Bob Marley said, 'If you smoke the herb, it will reveal you to yourself', and it is true. Only you know what you are really, alone with your own thoughts, and if you share the thoughts with someone, you truly trust them.

I notice the things that people do, not what they say; you learn to read people. The smallest favour is ten times better than the grandest of intentions. Some people will fuck your woman and rob you blind whilst patting you on the back and telling you how great you are, no moral compass whatsoever. If you're a big enough man to do that, you are big enough to pay the consequences. I had a friend who used to tell me he was Irish, and when they were debt collecting they would grab the guy who owed them money, take him into the woods and unearth a shallow grave, where a skeleton was, put a shotgun to his head and tell him, 'If the money is not paid ASAP, you are next!' They always paid up. It makes me laugh at that story, especially when somebody rips me off. I'm not like that, but if I were, I would call him.

When you travel alone all over London you are anonymous; if you're not in your village, at the tube station, where you reside that is. People are doing so many things; you don't have a clue what people are up to. I find it fascinating, there is so much depth and character in this city we call London. I have been coming to London since the 60s when my Uncle Barney lived in Islington and used to hang around with the big fat actor Arthur Mullard, who

I have since found out was abusing his daughter. Arthur Mullard, you never know about people, do you?

People do perk my intrigue. Some people, you just wonder what makes them tick, but you can guarantee it's usually down to their upbringing. We are all made up of our ancestors, all mixed in with our own foibles. We all sprang from the dawn of time, but most don't know much past their grandparents unless you are an aristocrat and are able to trace your roots back to the Norman Conquest or some such thing.

I truly love having a diverse bunch of friends. You learn so much from people. I have lived a purely hedonistic lifestyle, but I do relax and know how to wind down sometimes, otherwise I would have been dead years ago. I have many, many friends who have died over the years from drugs or alcohol, great lads who are no longer here with me. I have abused myself and pushed the boundaries, I make no bones about that. I have used drugs, but I don't let them use me; I know it sounds weird, but I do have a strong constitution and a strong mind. I know when to stop and I know not to do things 24/7, you open yourself up. I wouldn't encourage my body.

I came from the days of northern soul; I was exposed to drugs at a very early age. You can take heroin by smoking it, but as soon as you start injecting it, it can kill you. My advice, steer well clear; but there are many people who will not.

I first came across crack cocaine in New York. All the hookers were smoking it. I never really 'got it'. I kept trying it over the years, until one night when we spent £300 on it. My body was fucked, and I started to see then why it was so addictive, but steered clear of it, using it occasionally for a treat, until my heart attack. I knew my heart would give way if I carried on and I don't want to die just yet. In all my madness I can also be sensible, perhaps that's why I am still alive. Lots of junkies would use crack regularly and then smoke smack to bring them down off it, a deadly combination, but if you are into it, a great feeling.

I never went to rehab because I never felt the need to. I'm from the school of 'Rehab is for quitters.' Alcohol can be deadly, I've seen it destroy people up-close, friends, my family. I've had my spells with the booze too and paid the price many times.

I like Buddhism. Essentially, we are all our own gods and we know what is right and wrong. Nothing can be scientifically proven, you believe, or you don't. Like astrology, it truly makes more sense to me. The older you get you start to recognise certain qualities in people that you have seen in other people previously years before.

I am a very open-minded person. The more you travel, the more you read, the more experiences you garner, the more your mind is open to the world and your surroundings, recognising your own faults and inadequacies, and your qualities, and trying to work with what you have and do your best to be a better person. It's not easy but we're all striving for something. I want to learn and see things, and drugs have been part of my learning curve, rightly or wrongly, it is my life. I have hovered between life and death and not even noticed it.

I have been told many times I am lucky to be alive; there must be some purpose left in me. Maybe I'll pass something onto somebody before my journey on this earth ends. I have been with people many times and seen them in the same room die before my eyes. Their soul must leave them at that moment. Only a fool will think about death constantly, but it is inevitable. Perhaps people mask it by taking drugs or drinking, who knows, trying to stave it off.

Would I want my son to take drugs, or my daughter? NO! In the end, it is their choice, we all have choices, and some do, and some don't.

I have met highly intelligent people who can talk about everything and anything, but they have not been down my road and I have not been down theirs. We both have something to offer each other. People who read the *Guardian* or *The Times*, constantly quoting the day's news; read the same papers and you will know the same 'espousing' for all to hear. Research your own news, use your common sense with your intellect. Share your knowledge, not your bitterness or your faults, don't pass that on to your children, please.

I have seen people in their coffins. I have been around many deathbeds. What have I learned? That life really does go on. I still believe in people. You couple all these experiences together and I tell you this for a fact, live music gives you energy and makes you feel alive, you are connecting with something spiritual. Turn off the TV sets and read more, go and see live gigs, turn your radio on. Don't become old and jaded, forever complaining about everything. Yes, it's good to be interested and informed, but don't be brainwashed by the media telling you what music you should listen to and what clothes to wear, be an individual. Think for yourself. Travel and learn about the real world if you can, keep on learning, keep on loving, keep on being real. Don't be pretentious, be humble, care for your fellow man.

When you are down, the only way is up. Rock bottom is not a place I enjoy but it teaches you things about yourself. Maybe I unconsciously enjoy drama? When you are surrounded by it as a child, you need it in your life as you grow older, but I really have reached the stage where I hate it now.

I love music and parties; they take me to another plane. We all have many personalities. I think it helps me when I am working with musicians who have many different personalities, who knows?

When I was growing up, I had ginger hair, and they used to call me Tom Cat. Well, I have had nine lives, there must be somebody watching over me up above. I sometimes think after what I went through as a child, someone decided to help me have some fun later in my life because I really have had some fun, without a shadow of a doubt.

It's been a bit like sliding down a razor blade on my balls at times! When I was a small boy, I'd sit with men who had fought in World War Two, lapping up their stories of life, listening to them for hours.

I have always respected my elders and you should too: they have lived a life and if you listen to them you may just learn something. Now you go on, enjoy your own adventure, life truly is an adventure, and believe me, there is magic in the air.

'The purpose of our lives is to be happy'
                                            - Dalai Lama

Bye for now

About the Author

Tommy Kennedy IV was born in the North West of England. His early years were spent living in convents, caravans, and care homes around the UK.

He had a troubled childhood which resulted in him being sent to many institutions, before finally leaving his hometown and heading to the bright lights of London.

After a few years in London, he spent over a decade travelling the world, living off his wits and not much else.

His love of music saw him running a bar and putting parties on in Thailand, where he came into contact with many musicians on his travels and made the fateful decision to head back to Notting Hill in 1999, setting up a music promotions company. He spent over 4 years homeless through drink and drugs and going bankrupt and losing his home.

He has spent the last 21 years living in London's Notting Hill, where he managed and promoted bands, including managing Steve Dior, the legendary punk rock singer who was hanging out with and playing with Sid Vicious when he died in New York, and London rockers Pink Cigar, and from Warrington, Slydigs.

Driving bands around the UK, and across Europe, he was kept very busy. He has been working for the last 16 years on the world-famous Portobello Road, at the Mau Mau Bar, in Notting Hill, promoting gigs.

He has two children Sophie, and Tommy Jr, the lights of his life.

This is his second book. His first book, *Nightmare in Jamaica*, was published in August 2019 by New Haven Publishing.

His philosophy on life is 'find what you do best and share that knowledge to other people.'

Social Media Links

Email-tommykiv@gmail.com

Facebook-Justommy Nightmare in Jamaica

Twitter@tommykennedyiv

Linkedin -Tommy Kennedy IV

Instagram-Tommy Kennedy IV

www.newhavenpublishingltd.com

I appreciate any feedback on both of my books. Thanks for the reviews on Amazon, Goodreads, Waterstones. So far.

Tommy Kennedy IV London June 2020.

Here is a sample of Justommy first book available now

Chapter 1
Getting My Life Back

It was a steaming hot day in July 2003, and I was standing near the gate inside the prison walls of the notorious maximum-security unit of the General Penitentiary in Jamaica, when I heard a voice that startled me: 'Don't forget, white man, when you get back to England, you tell everybody I'm an innocent man.' I realised it was Leppo, convicted of three murders in 1987, including that of reggae superstar Peter Tosh and his friends. All I could think was, *Get me the fuck out of here!*

I had just completed my sentence, over 700 nights, during which I had witnessed many murders, a vast amount of beatings and stabbings, and met some heavy duty Yardies who would, and have, cut people's throats in the blink of an eye. Members of the shower posse, who used Uzi submachine guns, so named for the way they would rain a shower of bullets down on their victims. Their leader Christopher Coke had ruthlessly used a chainsaw to dismember one of a gang who had stolen drugs from him.... while he was still alive, the rest of the Shower Posse looking on laughing while the guy died screaming in agony. You did not fuck around with these guys if you valued your life.

Eventually, the police turned up to take me to the airport. Even then I was never sure if I was getting out. When the gates swung open and we drove through, I smiled to myself and gave a brief wave to Leppo as we left him standing, glaring at the departing police van. We arrived at the airport to find out my plane had been delayed.

Fuck, they stuck me in a holding cell at the airport in Kingston until I got on a plane! I wasn't really sure if this was going to happen; I started getting paranoid, maybe it was a wind-up. Eventually, my time came to board. They led me handcuffed until I was let onto the plane and the stewardess took over. As we

178

took off, I thought of all the days when I used to see the British Airways flights leaving Kingston, heading from Jamaica to the UK, which I used to watch from my prison cell regularly (mental torture). And now, finally, at last, I was on the plane, leaving. The stewardess greeted me with 'Welcome aboard' and gave me a wink; she could see how happy I was to be leaving police custody. I winked back and said 'Nice one.'

I breathed a huge sigh of relief whilst ordering a beer off the good-looking stewardess and thinking, *Yes! Got my life back, on to further adventures and god knows what else.* But I also remember pondering: *Whatever happens from here on it can only be up after this.* Little did I know what lay ahead. All I knew was I had to get back to London to resume my passion for music. This had become all-consuming and gave me a purpose, something that had been lacking for so many years in my life. By the time we landed at Manchester airport and I cleared customs after a two-hour grilling by immigration officers, I was buzzing. I stepped out into the English summer and the first person I saw was my younger brother Anthony, who stuck a camera in my face and took a photo. I looked a right twat, none of my clothes fit, my hair was down my back, but I didn't give a toss, I was out, I was free! We hugged, and our Anthony said, 'Long time no see.' I got down on my knees and kissed the ground, and we both laughed. Man, was I happy to be on home turf.

The only good thing about prison is the day they let you out. It beats all the birthdays and Christmases, nothing better than getting your freedom back. It's almost worth the experience just to have that feeling when they set you free. Anyway, we jumped into our kid's car and headed back to my hometown of Warrington, where he still lived at the time with his wife Paula and their kids, Alfie and Mia. This was Anthony's second marriage and they seemed really happy together.

I hadn't sat on a toilet or had a bath in over two years. It was heaven soaking in the bath and using a proper toilet. Our kid gave me some money and some new clothes to wear. He really is a star and I love him dearly, even though he can drive me crazy at times; we are brothers and I love him unconditionally. We had food and Paula made me feel welcome; it had not been easy for the family with the situation I had landed myself in, they had been worried about my safety.

Later that night my cousin Jack turned up and we had a few beers and a laugh about the predicament I had just been through. I didn't want to dwell on it just yet and caught up on all the news. It turned out Jack had been hanging around with Noel Gallagher from Oasis for a few years before he became famous. They had met from the rave days many years before at the Hacienda. Our Jack was like a brother to me. His mum and my mum were sisters, and both loved each other's company, so as kids we were always together. Noel always puts him on the guest list of various gigs, and they are still in contact over 25 years later. Jack and Noel still text each other, although he is quite shy and not one for bothering people, including me. Jack is five years my junior and very respected in Warrington. He gave me some cash and said, 'Spend it wisely' when he departed later that night.

The next day I went and saw my dad, who has been a constant throughout my life. He always did his best by me, along with my sister Lynn, and our Anthony. My dad had joined the Merchant Navy when he was 16 and spent 12 years sailing around the world in the 50s and 60s, later regaling us with stories of exotic places. It was through my father that my love of travel came. All through my school days, the only thing I wanted to do was join the Navy and see the world, but sadly it was not meant to be. From 13 to 21 I hit a rebellious streak and spent most of it in detention centres, Borstal and prisons around the country. I applied for the Merchant Navy and the Royal Navy numerous times, but with my criminal record, it was a no-go!

It was great to see my dad. He had given up the booze at the age of 52 after a lifetime of boozing, which I was thankful for, or else he would have died. We hugged, and he gave me some money. I was totally broke when they let me out and was really thankful. One of my good friends, Liz, came over and also gave me some money. Liz was a great girl and a good friend; she is now living in Australia, and I wish her all the best. I had met her when she was on the front desk of Legends night club in Warrington, taking the door money. I think she liked my cheek, and I amused her. Her brother Sean started Legends in the early 90s! Legends was at the forefront of house music in Warrington, and people flocked there from all over the UK.

Liz was a nurse and had a caring nature at the best of times, but she did a great job dealing with people, and Legends was making so much money it was packed every weekend. Gangsters started coming from Manchester issuing death threats to her brother Sean, threatening to blow his car up if they couldn't get in on the action, but fair play to Sean, he took it all in his stride and went on to put Legends on the map, big time. Scousers and Mancs were always coming to Warrington for the nightlife; some carried guns and knives, but the Warrington crew were just as bad and never backed down from them. After a few days I realised I had to get back to London: I was missing the buzz of city life and I knew Warrington only spelled trouble for me. So, after a few goodbyes and laughs with family, I hitched a ride with Eny, an old school friend who lived in Canary Wharf and was quite successful. I'd always admired him: he took the straight road and studied hard, and now he lives in Qatar and has done really well for himself. We are like chalk and cheese, but we are mates and always have a laugh when we meet up.

I had nowhere to live when I arrived in London. One of the Jamaicans who I met in the General Penitentiary, Carrot, had a flat in Brixton and told me to go there. Eny dropped me off and I knocked on the door. A woman came down and I explained who I was. Next thing I was upstairs with her and three Jamaican guys who took an instant dislike to me. I stayed there and nearly had a brief affair with the Jamaican woman, but I think the guys got wind of it and kicked me out after about a month.

Luckily my good mate from Warrington, Rob Taylor, rang me. He lived in Ladbroke Grove and told me his mate had a flat with a box-room on Westbourne Park Road, just off Portobello, £50 a week. Fuck, there is a god! I was no stranger to London. I had lived all over it since the early 80s and had been living around the Grove for a few years before I got nicked in Jamaica. Tony, who I moved into the flat with, was a man after my own heart, intelligent, a heart of gold, born and bred around the Grove, and better still, the local drug dealer. Fuck, we hit it off from the moment we met. Let's have a beer he said, and we hit The Castle on the corner of Portobello Road that used to be called The Warwick, Joe Strummer's boozer from the Clash back in the day.

I love London. Having lived all over the country and travelled all around the world, I've lived in many countries, but this is a special city: 300 languages are spoken, people are here from every corner of the globe and there's a buzz in the air. The summertimes are wicked in London. I'm learning to appreciate the winters too. I was born in wintertime, October 16th; wow, I'm still here when so many of my friends and family are dead and buried.

'I'm in love with cities I've never been to and people I have never met.' John Green

Next Project:

One of the most fascinating serial killers that I heard about in the 70s was Charles Sobhraj when I was travelling throughout Asia. Half Vietnamese and Indian, who lived in both Asia and France, he preyed on his victims across South East Asia in the 1970s. They were mainly western tourists in search of spiritual guidance, seduced and entranced by Sobhraj who ultimately led them to their deaths. He served a life sentence in India and was released and sent back to France, a serial killer who could not resist the lure of the orient a few years later he went back and was arrested in Nepal where he is currently serving a second life sentence. A charismatic psychopath, who has been the subject of 4 books and documentaries. He will be the subject of my next book.

9 781912 587346